GB Graphics Presents
Hans Holbein's

Dance
of
Death

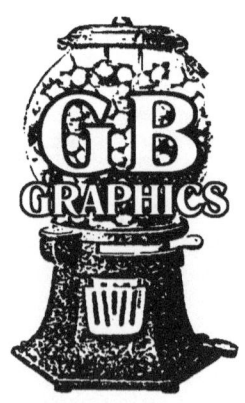

Presented here are the 49 woodcuts of Hans Holbein's Dance of Death as presented in Bohn's Illustrated Library: Holbein's Dance of Death (1858).

However for accuracy, plates 40-47 are not thought to have actually been done by Holbein and were added to the group after the original publication in 1538.

I.
THE CREATION

The Deity is seen taking Eve from the side of Adam.

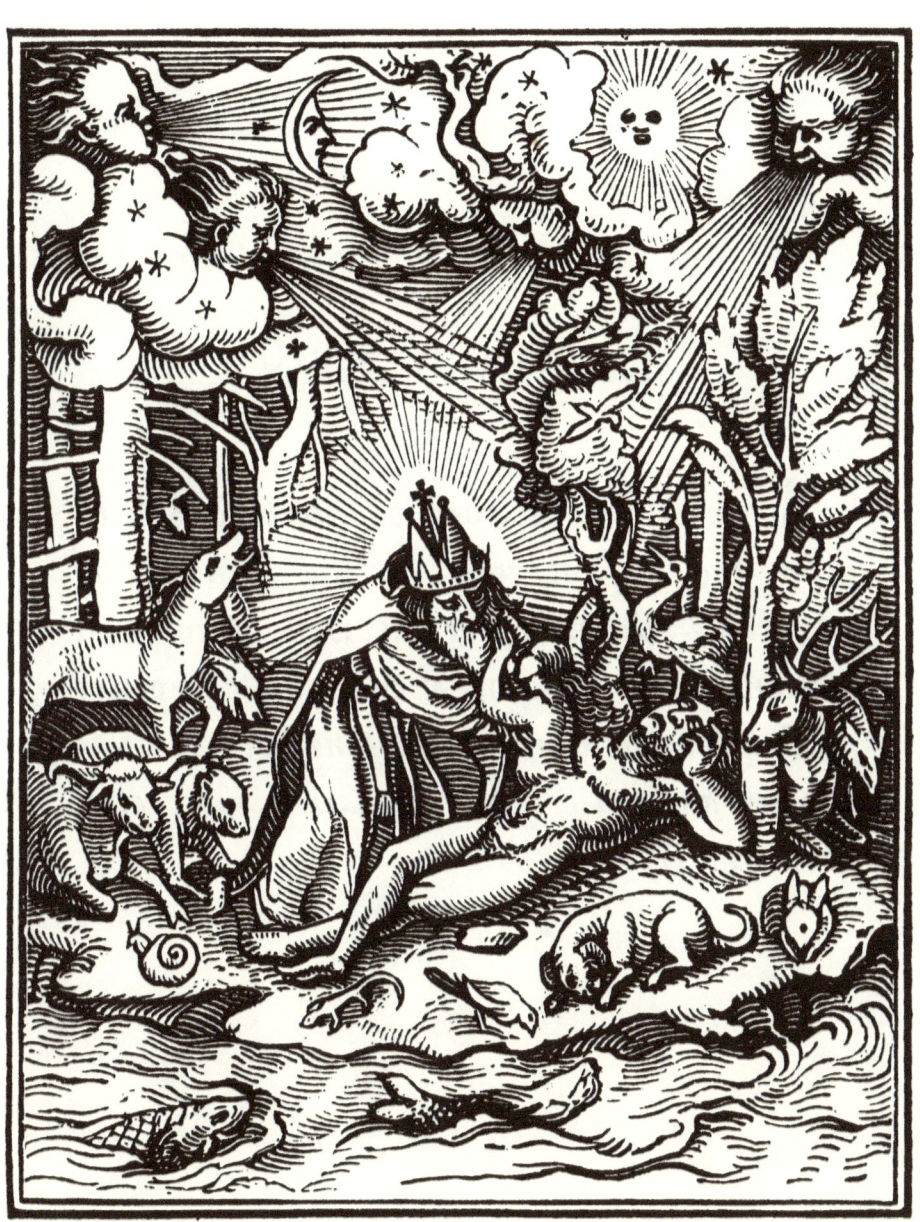

II.
THE TEMPTATION

Eve has just received the forbidden fruit from the serpent, who, on the authority of venerable Bede, is her, as well as in most ancient representations of the subject, depicted with a female human face. She holds it up to Adam, and entices him to gather more of it from the tree.

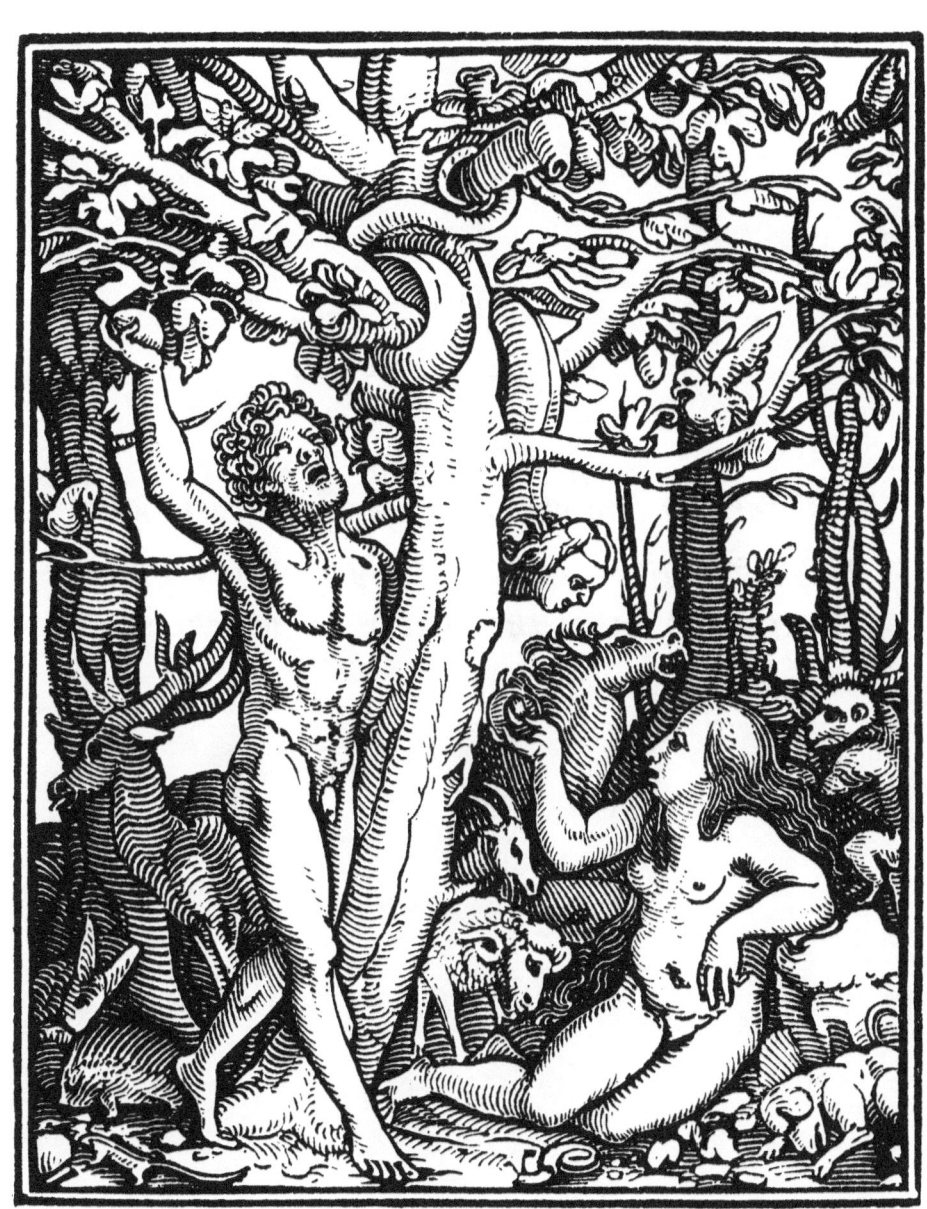

III.
THE EXPULSION

Adam and Eve are preceded by Death, who plays on a vielle, or beggar's lyre, as if demonstrating his joy at the victory he has obtained over man.

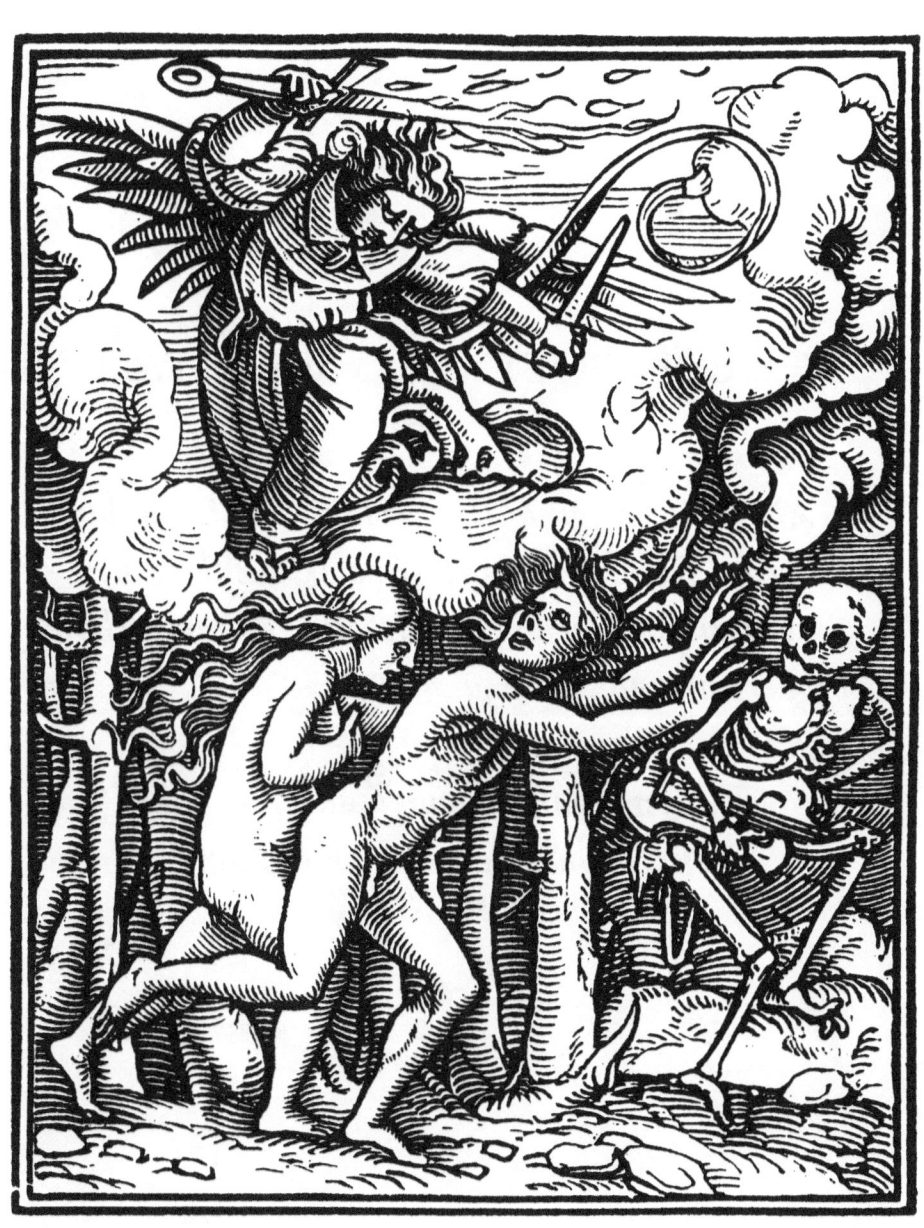

IV.
THE CONSEQUENCES OF THE FALL

Adam is digging the ground, assisted by Death. In the distance Eve is suckling her first-born, and holding a distaff. Whence the proverb in many languages:

When Adam Delved and Eve span,
Where was then the gentleman?

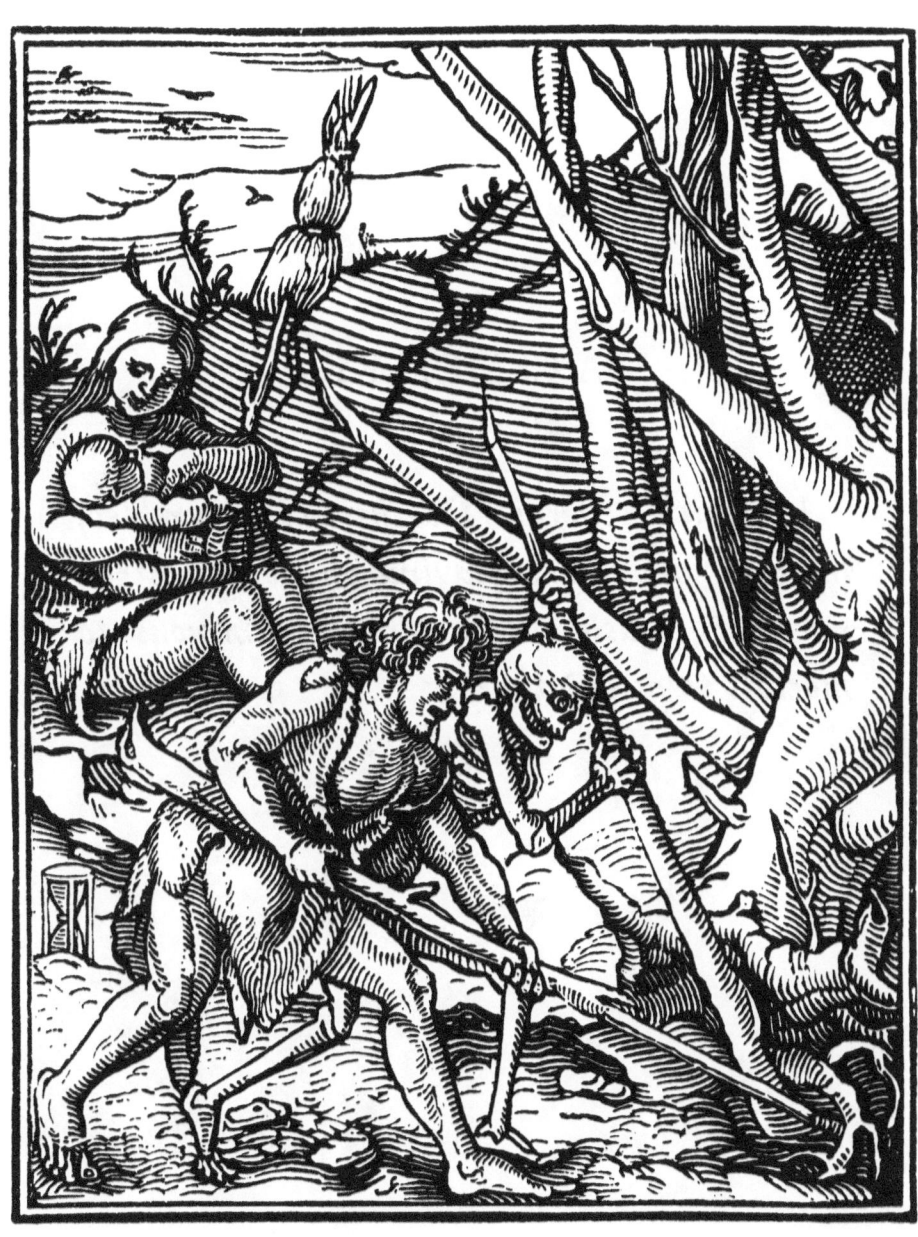

V.
A CEMETERY

In which several Deaths are assembled, most of whom are playing on noisy instruments of music, as a general summons to mortals to attend them.

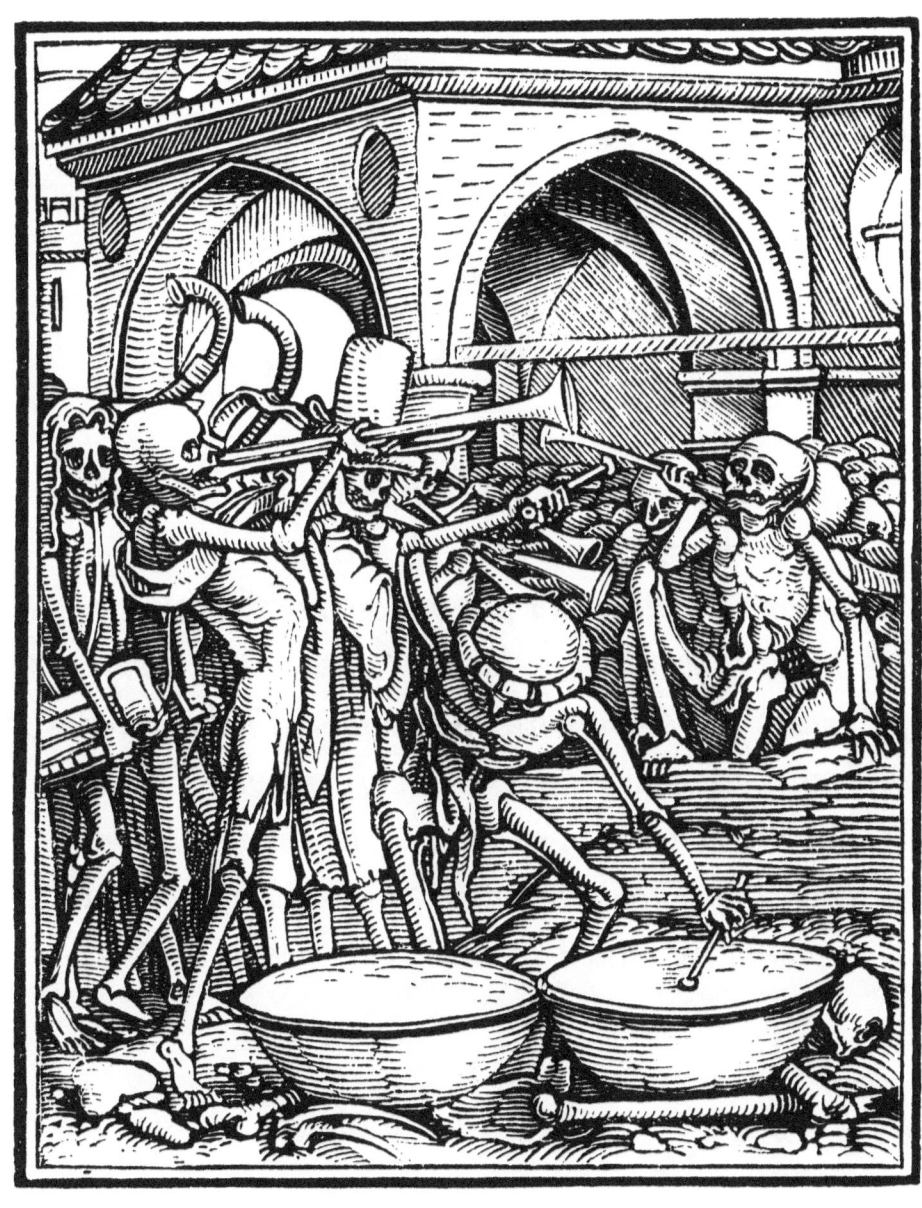

VI.
THE POPE

He is crowning an Emperor, who kneels before him, two Cardinals attending, one of whom is ludicrously personated by Death. In the background are bishops etc. Death embraces the Pope with one hand, with the other leans on a crutch. Two grotesque Devils are introduced into the cut, one whom hovers over the Pope; the other, in the air, holds a diploma, to which several seals are appended.

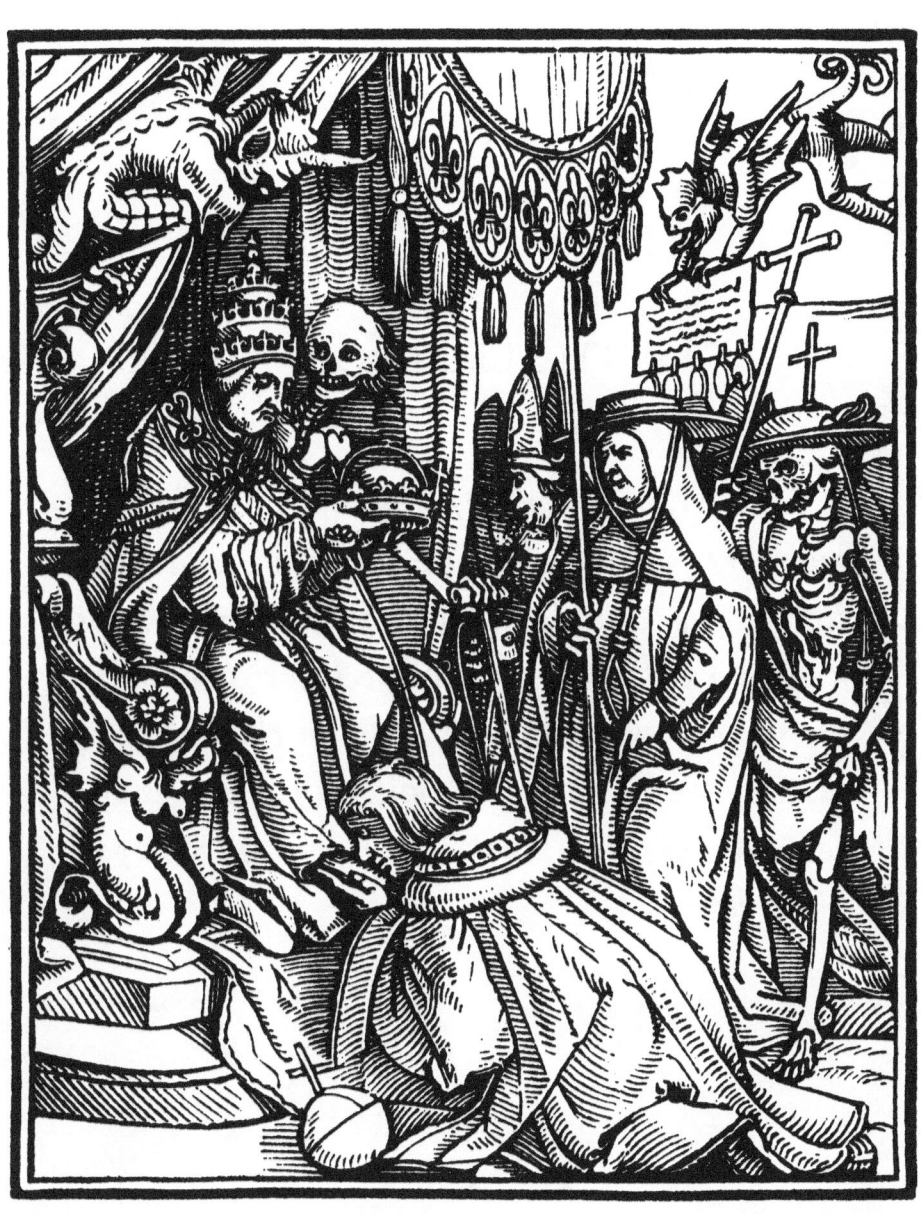

VII.
THE EMPEROR

Seated on a throne, and attended by his courtiers, he seems to be listening to, or deciding, the complaint of a poor man who is kneeling before him, against his rich oppressor, whom the Emperor, holding the sword of justice, seems to regard with an angry countenance. Behind him Death lays hands upon his crown.

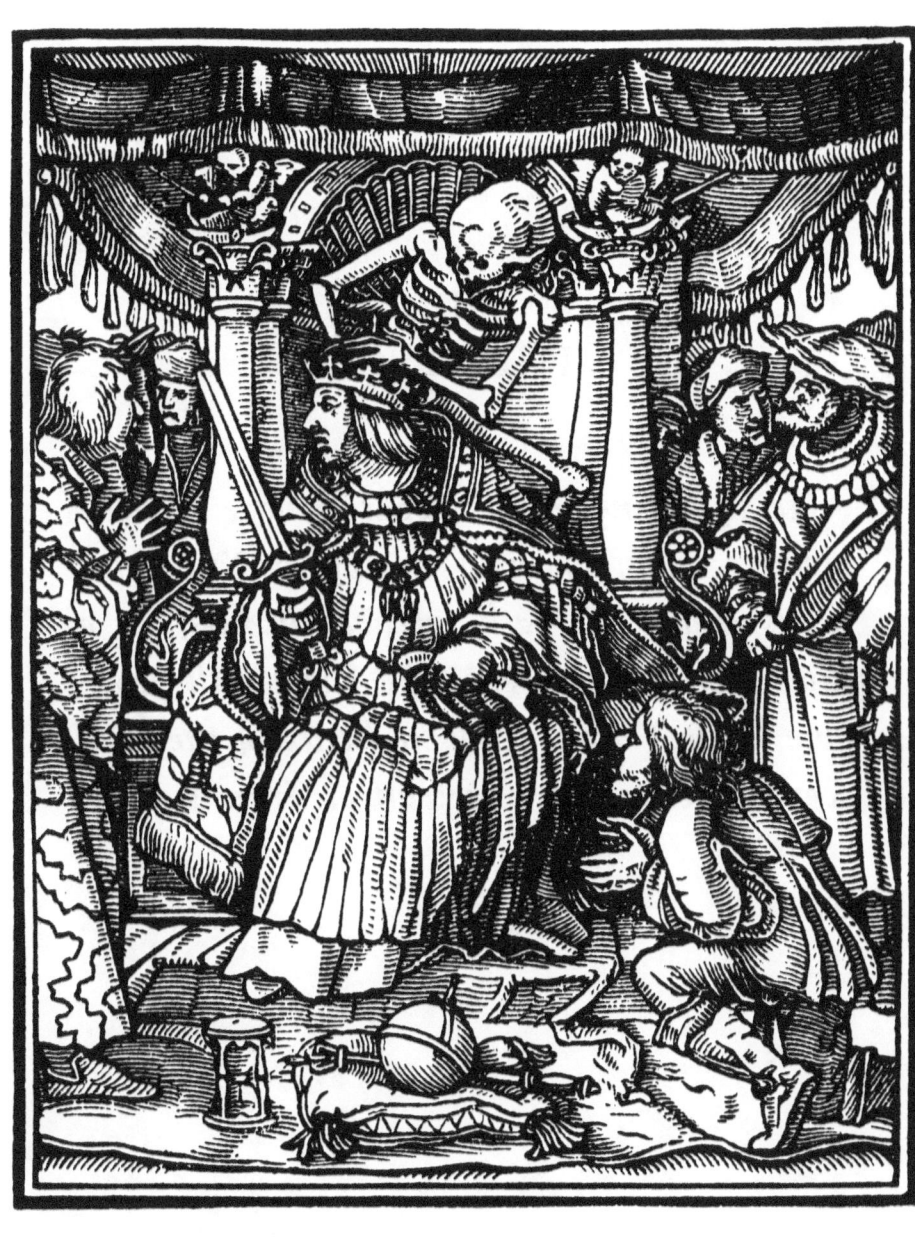

VIII.
THE KING

He is sitting at his repast before a well-covered table, under a canopy studded with fleurs-de-lis. Death intrudes himself as a cupbearer, and presents the King with probably his last draught. The figure of the king seems intended as a portrait of Francis I.

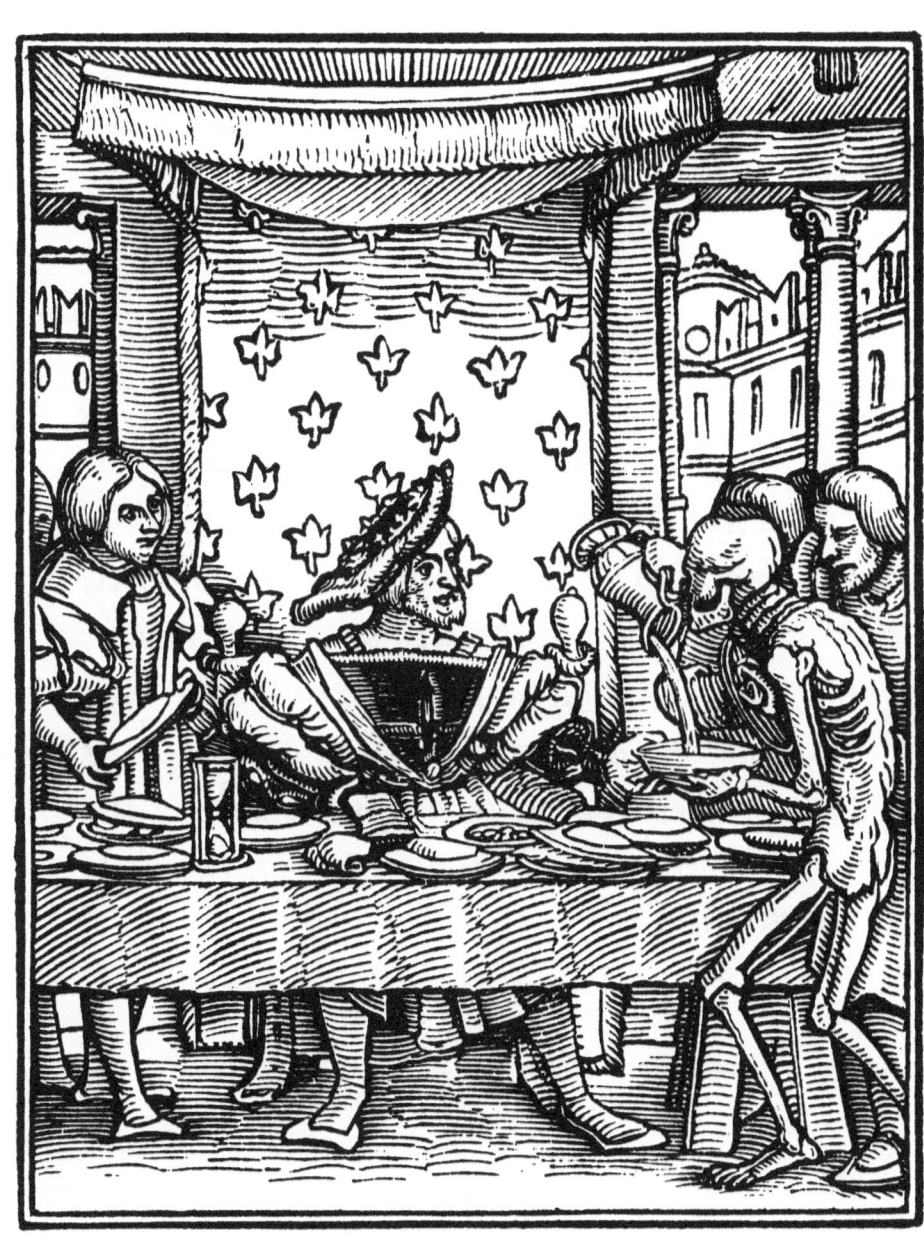

IX.
THE CARDINAL

There is some difficulty in ascertaining the real meaning of the designer of this subject. It has been described as the Cardinal receiving the bull of his appointment, or as a rich man making a purchase of indulgences. The latter interpretation seems warranted by the Latin motto. Death is twisting off the Cardinal's hat.

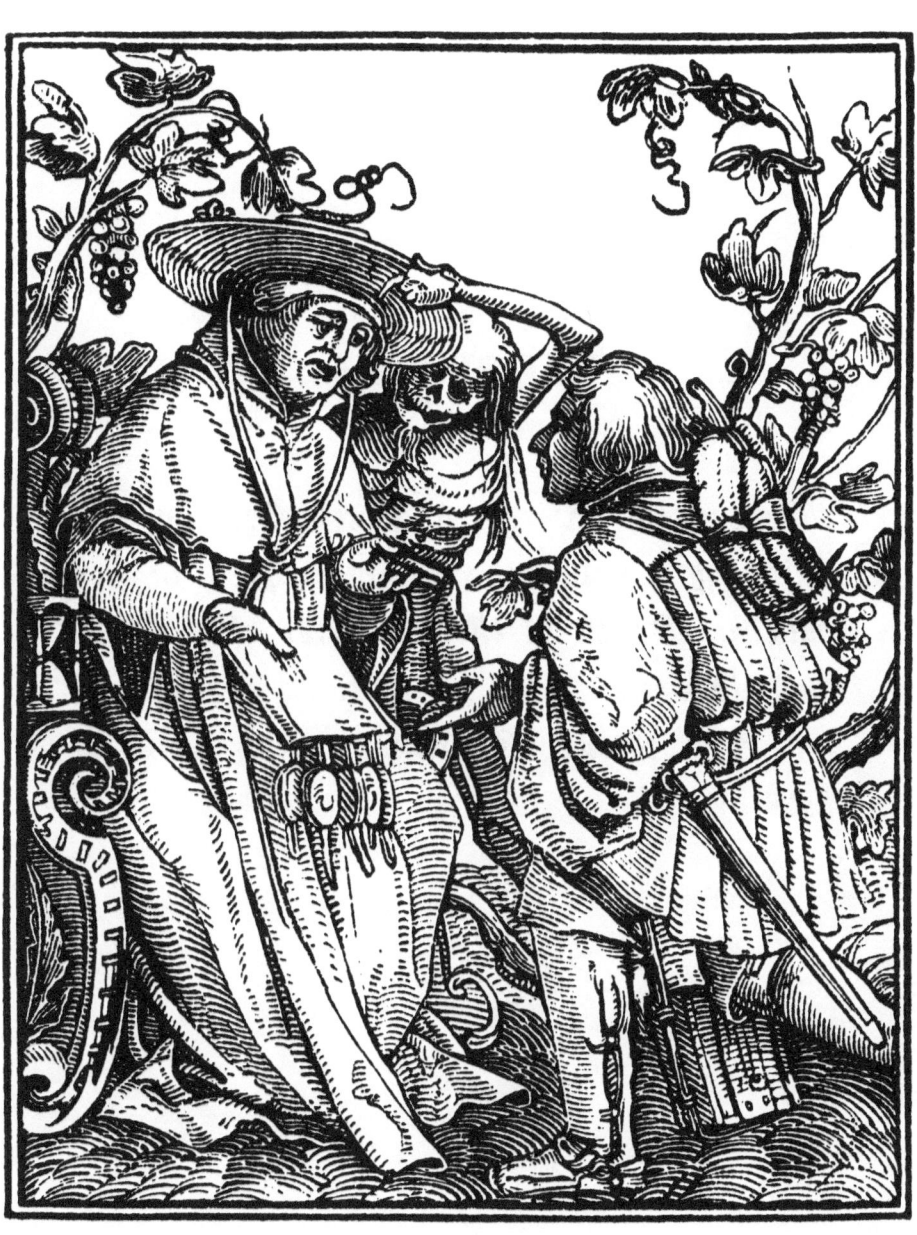

X.
THE EMPRESS

Gorgeously attired and attended by her maids of honour, she is intercepted in her walk of Death in the character of a shrivelled old woman, who points to an open grave, and seems to say, "To this you must come at last."

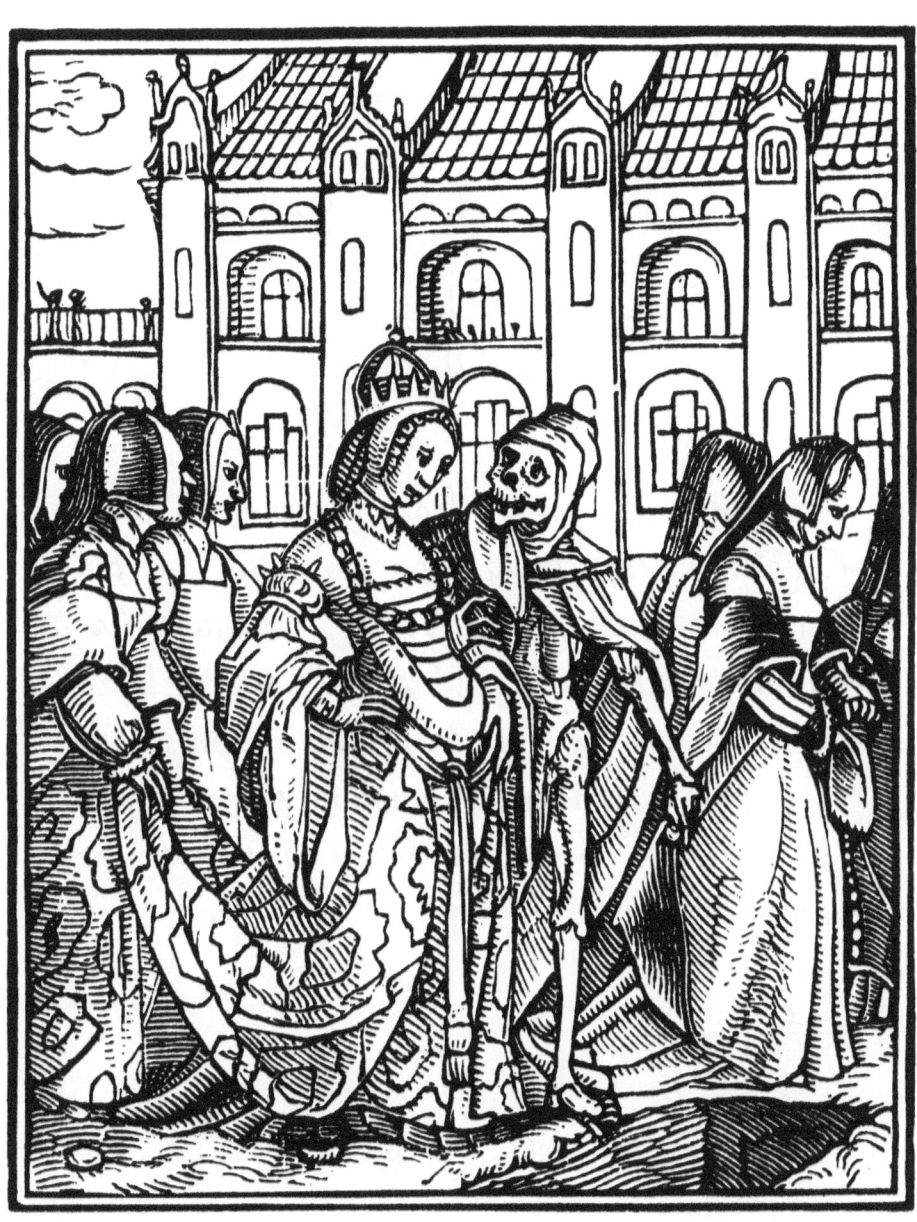

XI.
THE QUEEN

She has just issued from her palace, when Death unexpectedly appears and forcibly drags her away. Her Jester, in whose habiliments Death has ludicrously attired himself, endeavors in vain to protect his mistress. A female attendant is violently screaming. Death holds up his hour-glass to indicate the arrival of the fatal hour.

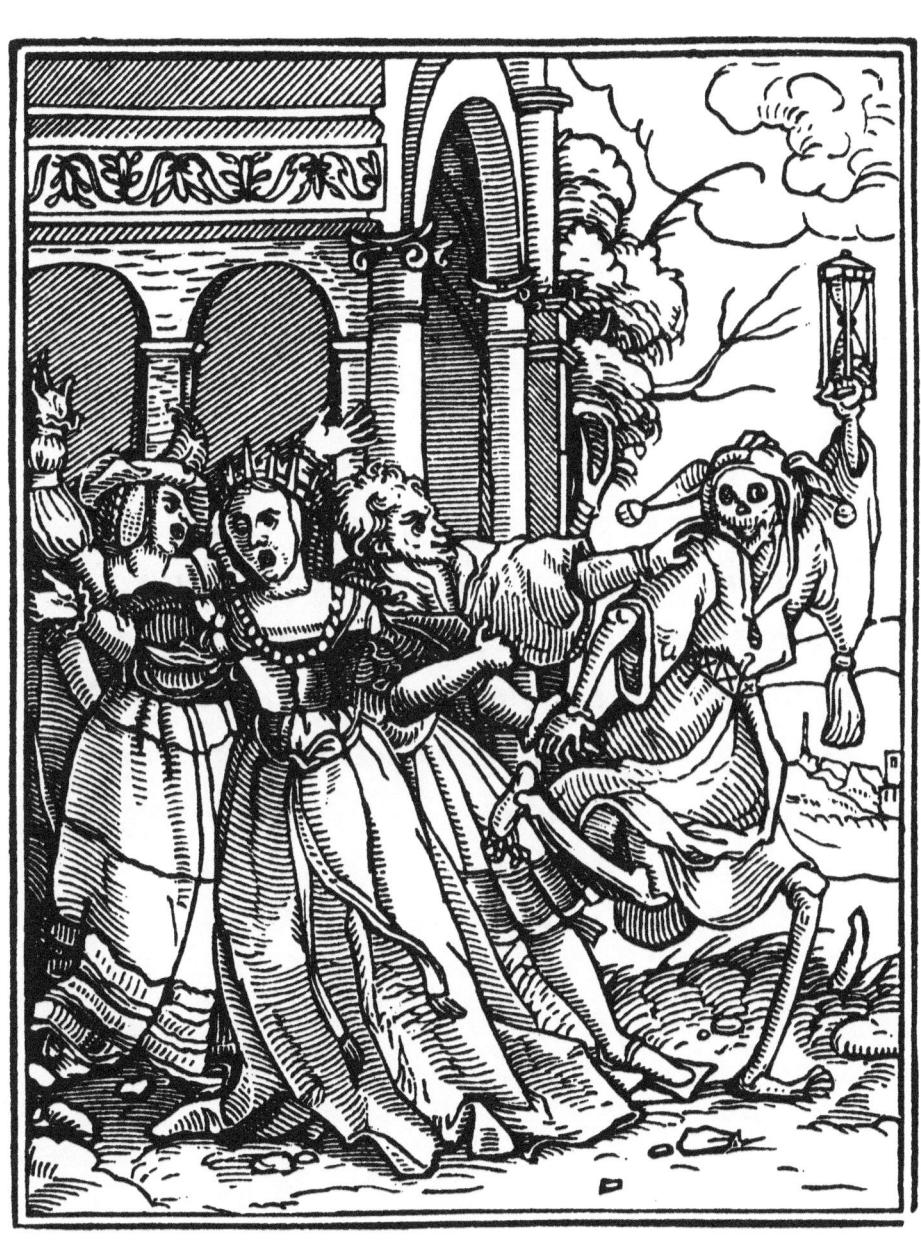

XII.
THE BISHOP

Quietly resigned to his fate he is led away be Death, whilst the loss of the worthy Pastor is symbolically deplored by the flight and terror of several shepherds in the distance amidst their flocks. The setting sun is very judiciously introduced.

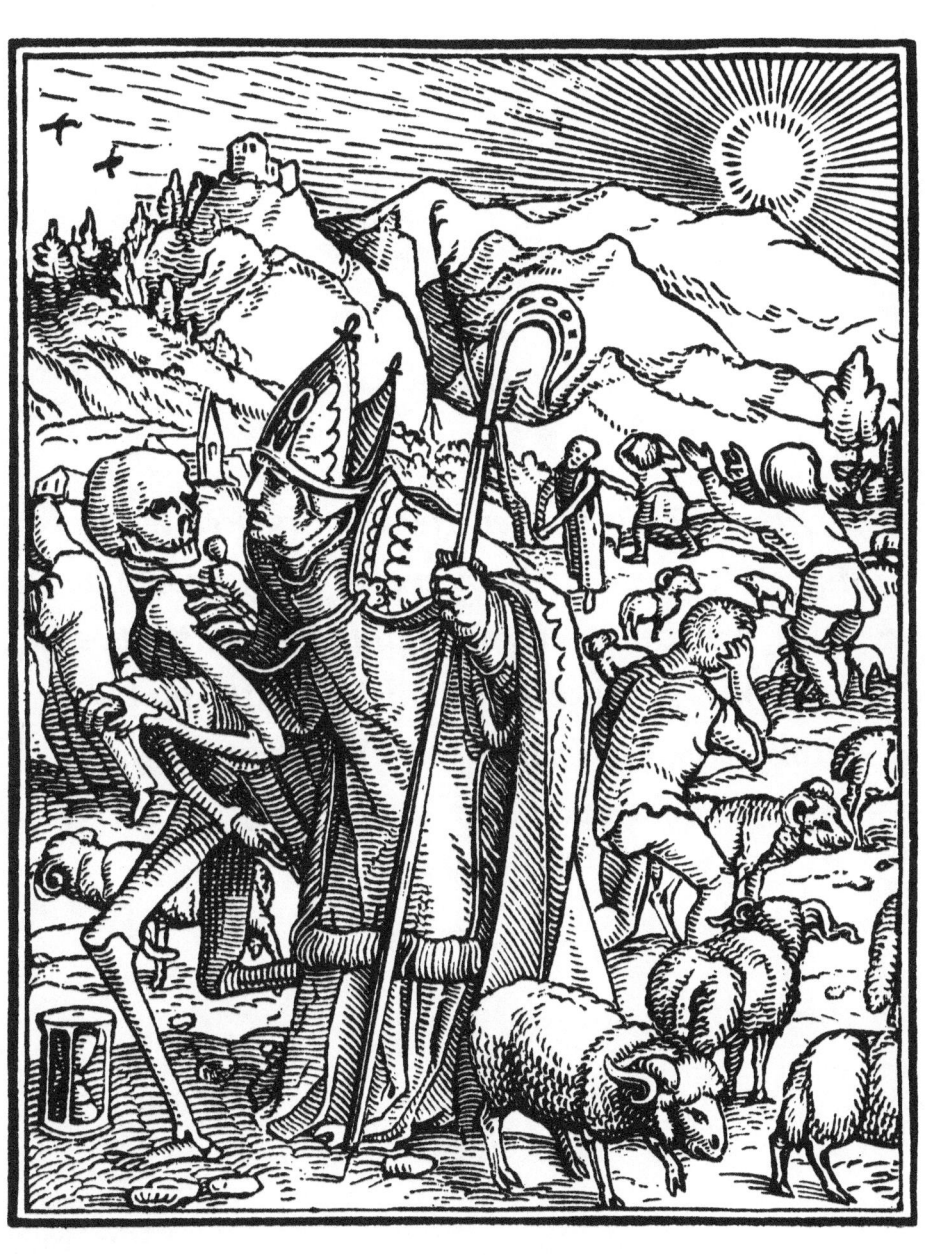

XIII.
THE DUKE

Attended by his courtiers, he is accosted in the street for charity by a poor beggar woman with her child. He disdainfully turns aside from her supplication, whilst Death, fantastically crowned with leaves, unexpectedly lays violent hands upon him.

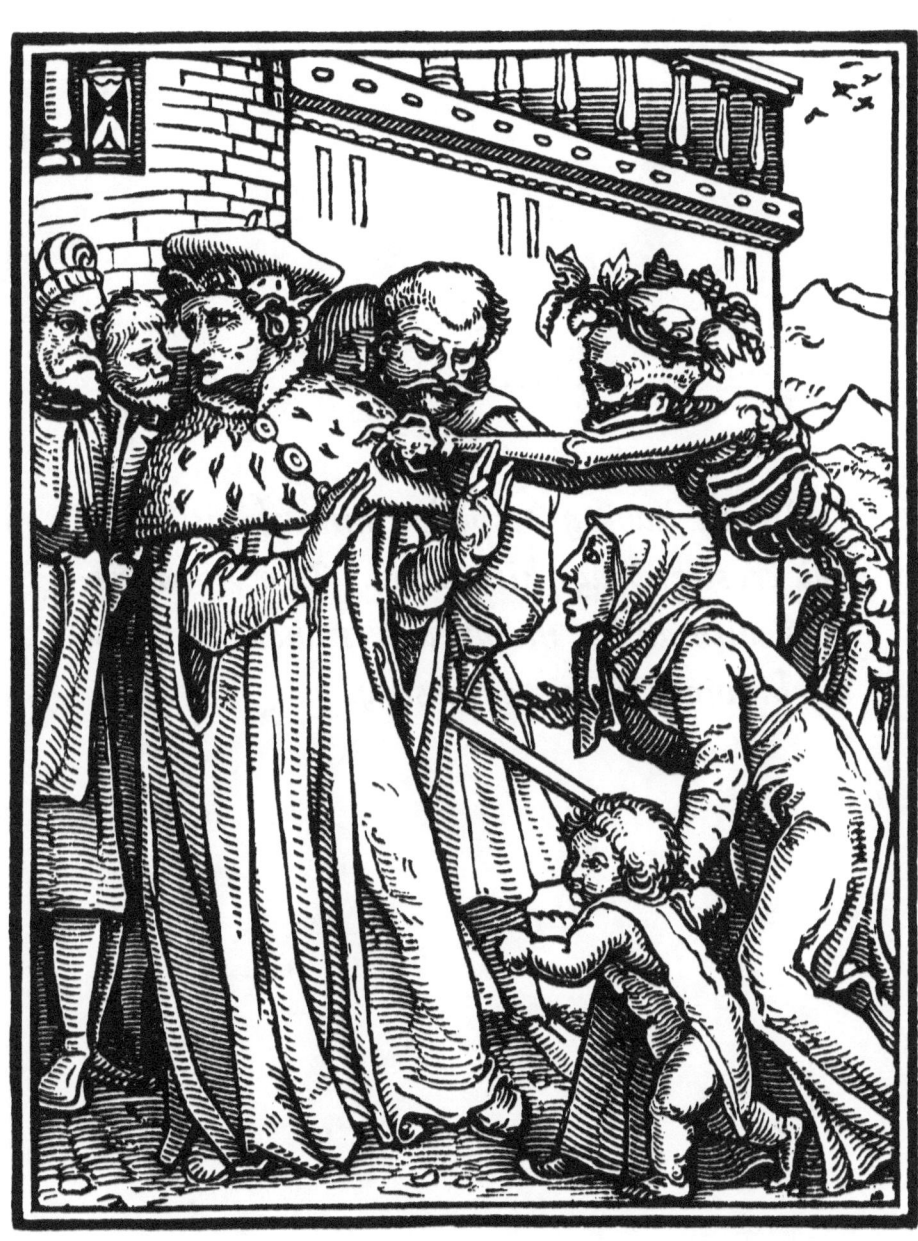

XIV.
THE ABBOT

Death having despoiled him of his mitre and crosier, drags him away. The Abbot resists with all his might, and is about to throw his breviary at his adversary.

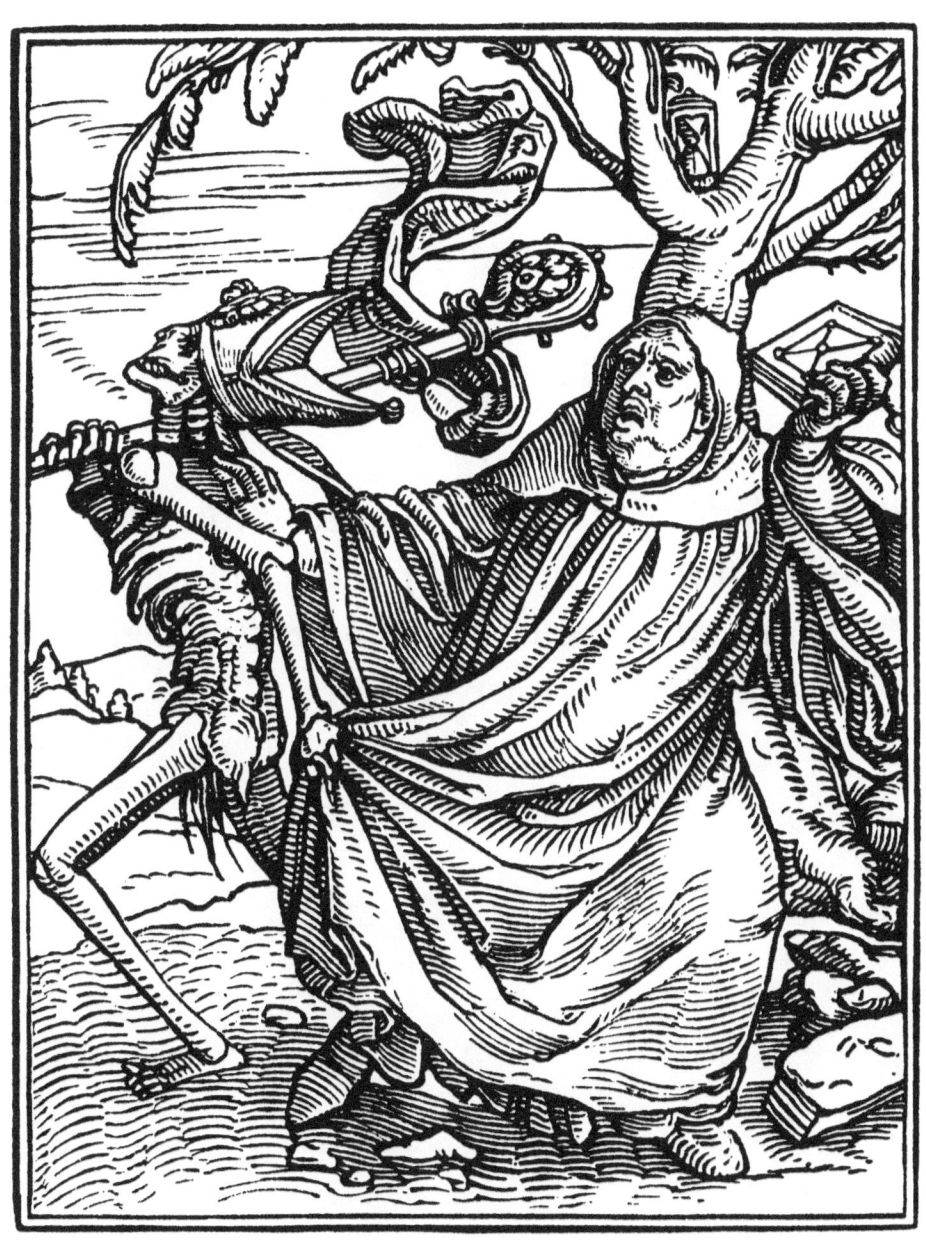

XV.
THE ABBESS

Death, grotesquely crowned with flags, seizes the poor Abbess by her scapulary. A Nun at the convent gate, with uplifted hands, bewails the fate of her superior.

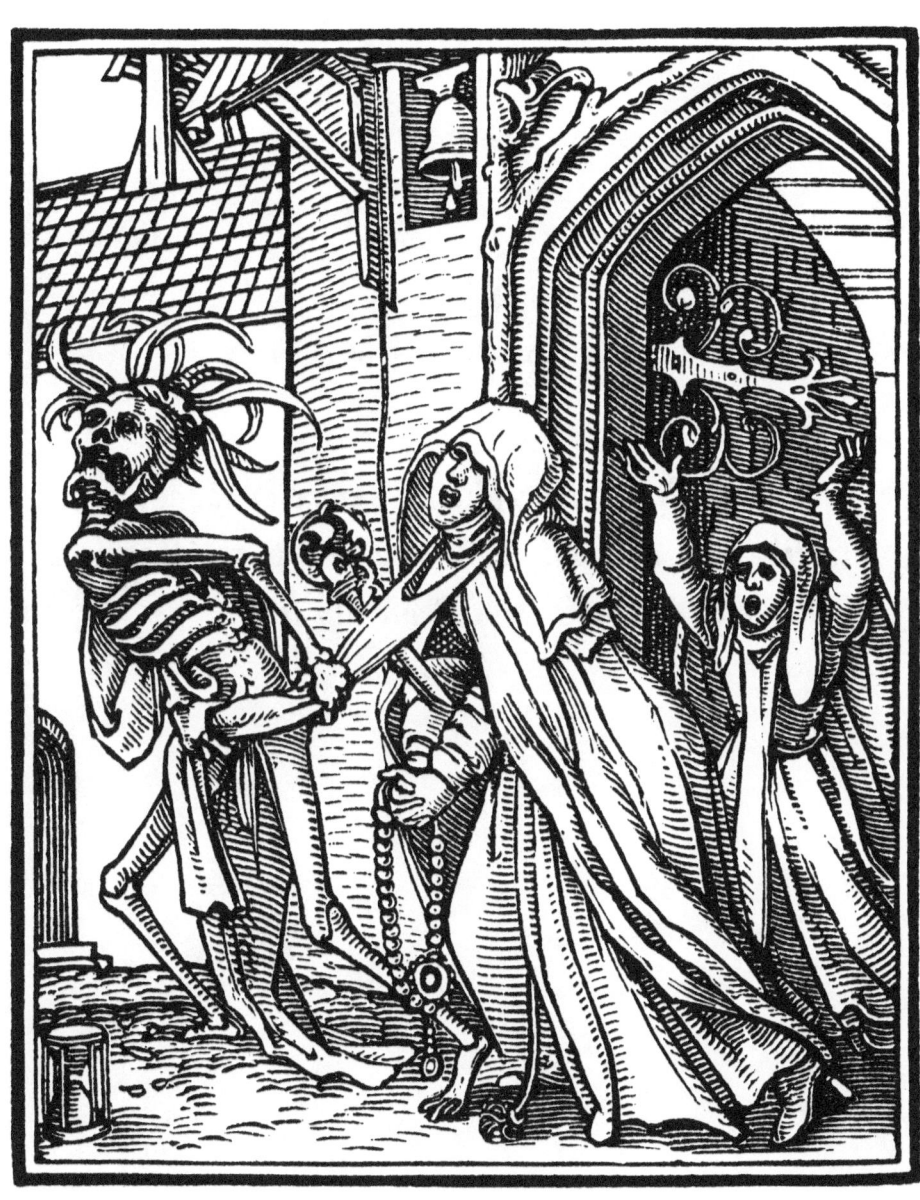

XVI.
THE GENTLEMAN

He vainly, with uplifted sword, endeavours to liberate himself from the grasp of Death. The hour-glass is placed on his bier.

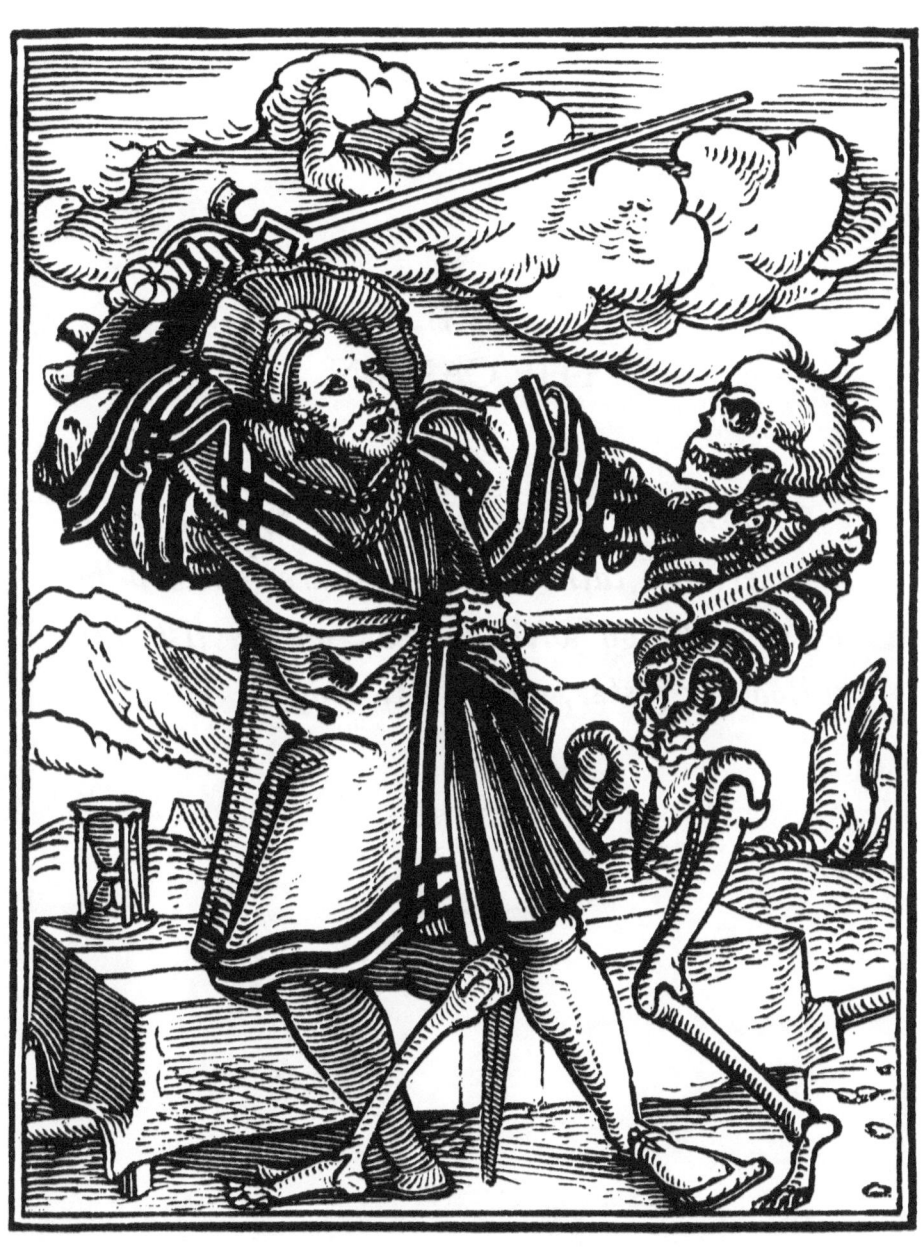

XVII.
THE CANON

Death hold up his hour-glass to him as he is entering a cathedral. They are followed by a noble person with a hawk on his fist, his buffoon or jester, and a little boy.

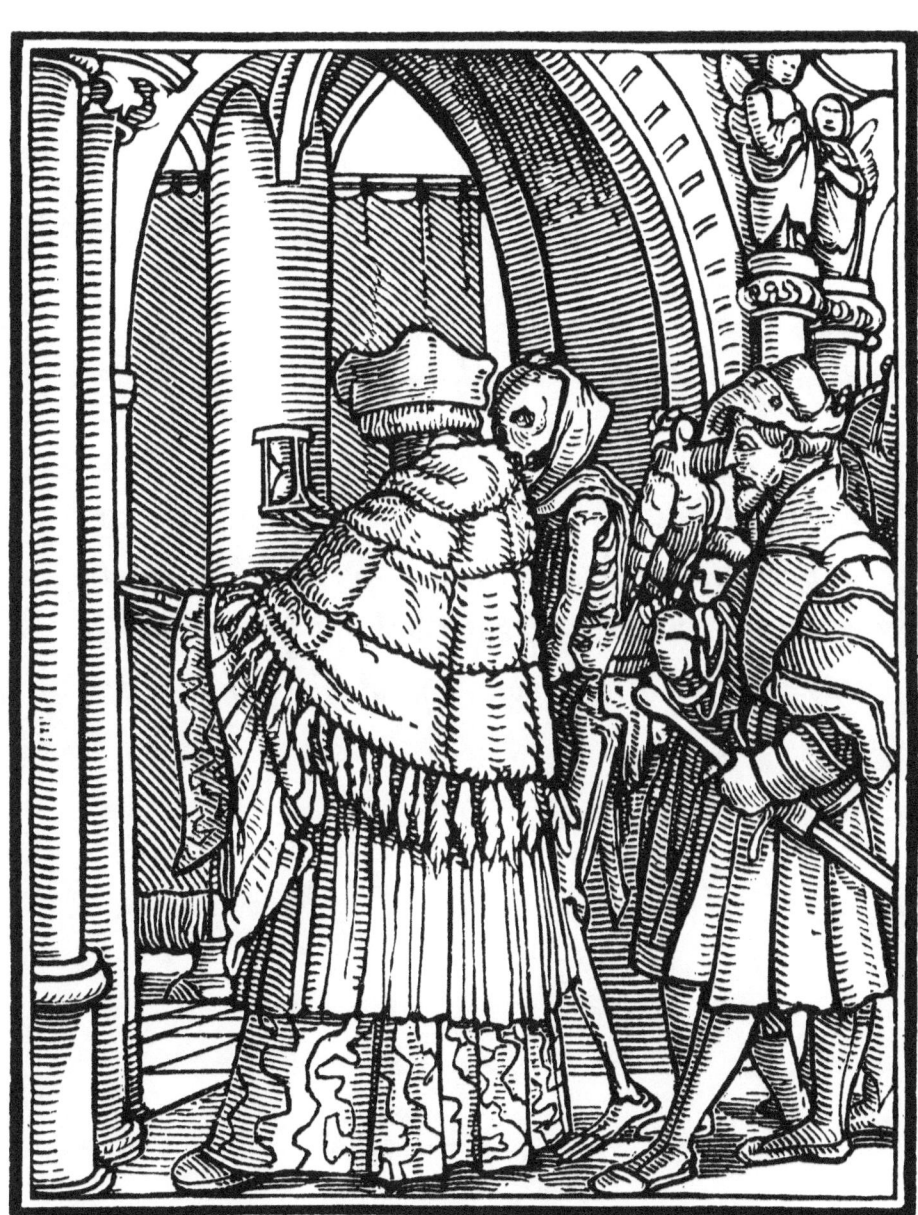

XVIII.
THE JUDGE

He is deciding a cause between a rich and a poor man. From the former he is about to receive a bribe. Death behind him snatches his staff of office from one of his hands.

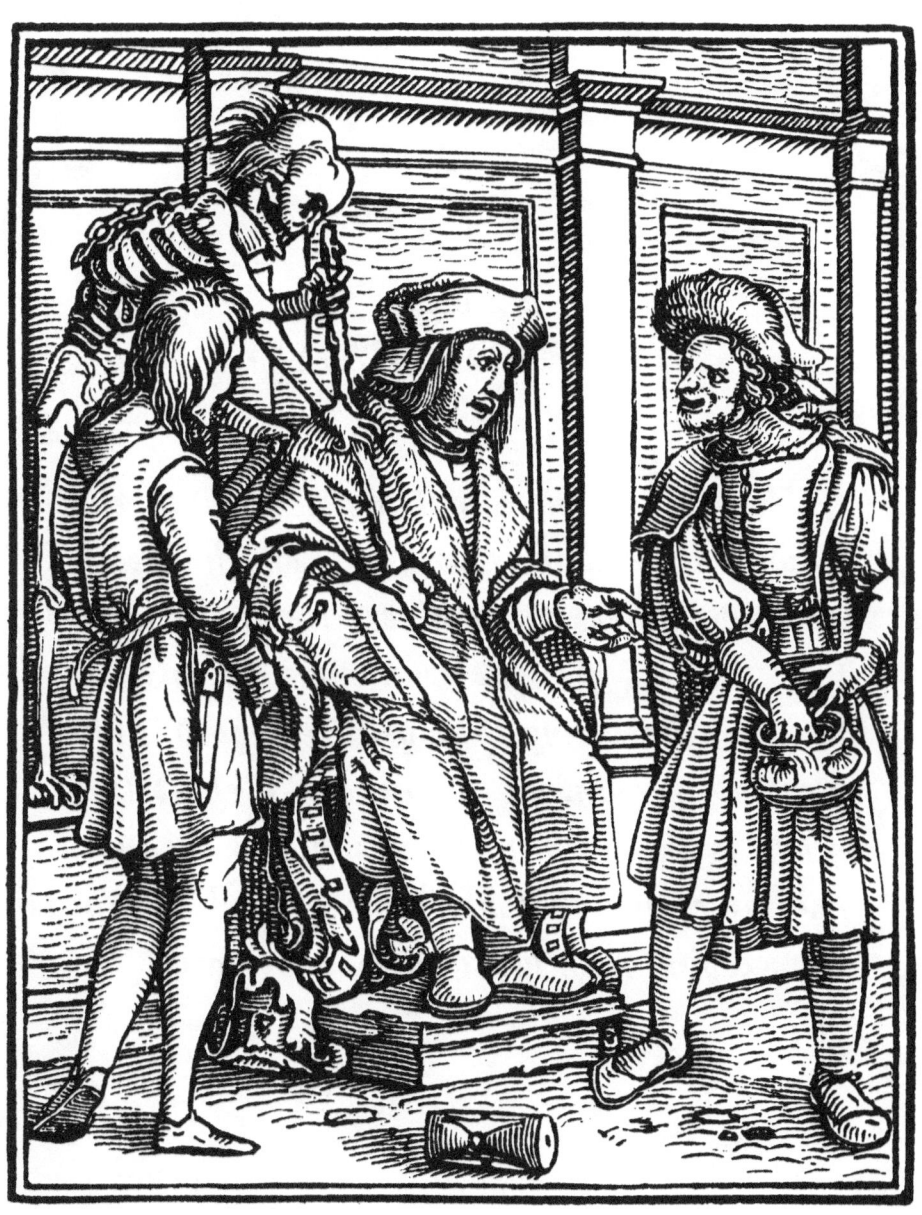

XIX.
THE ADVOCATE

The rich client is putting a fee into the hands of the dishonest lawyer, to which Death also contributes, but reminds him at the same time that his glass has run out. To this admonition he seems to pay little regard, fully occupied in counting his money. Behind this group is the poor suitor, wringing his hands, and lamenting that his poverty disables him from coping with his wealthy adversary.

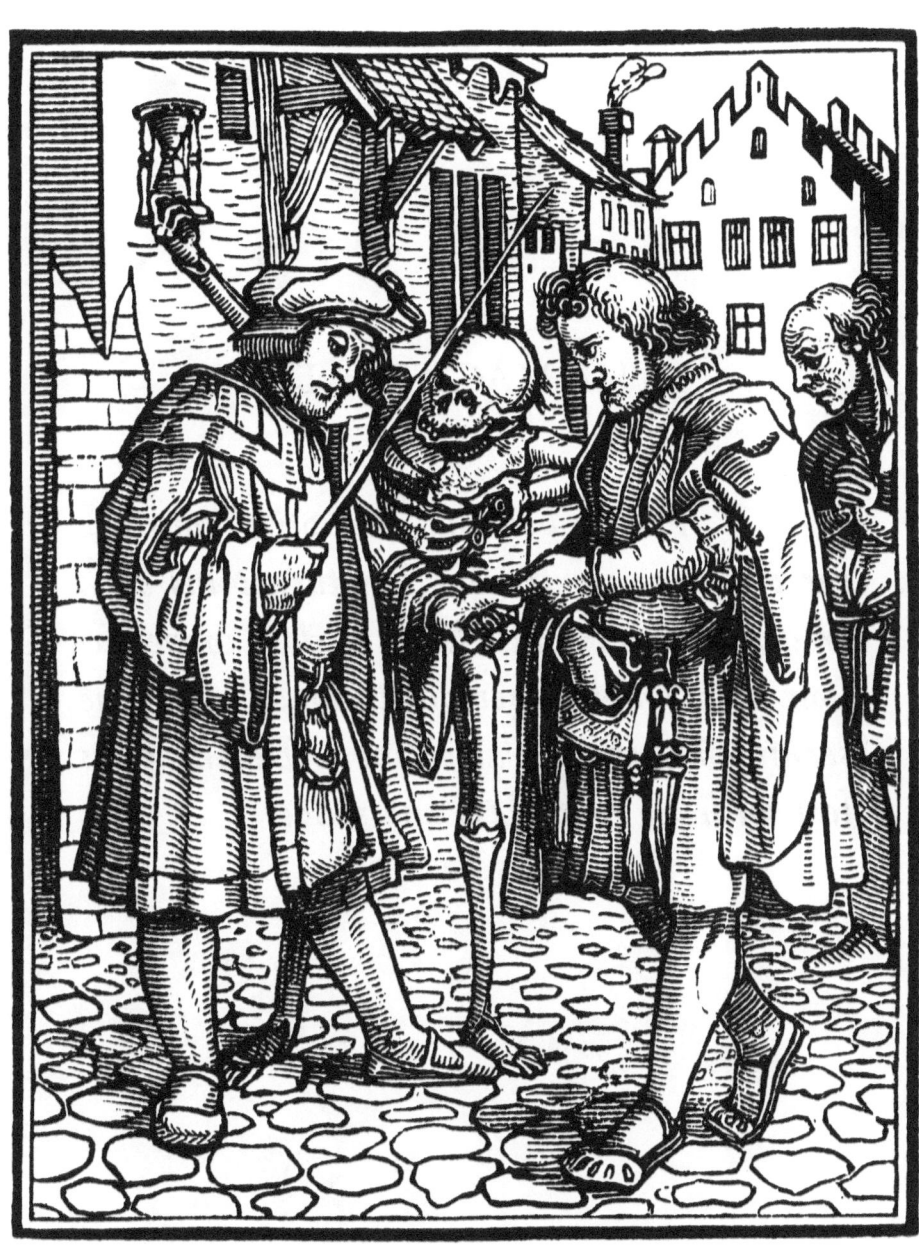

XX.
THE MAGISTRATE

A Demon is blowing corruption into the ear of a magistrate, who has turned his back on a poor man, whilst he is in close conversation with another person, to whose story he seems emphatically attentive. Death at his feet with an hour-glass and spade.

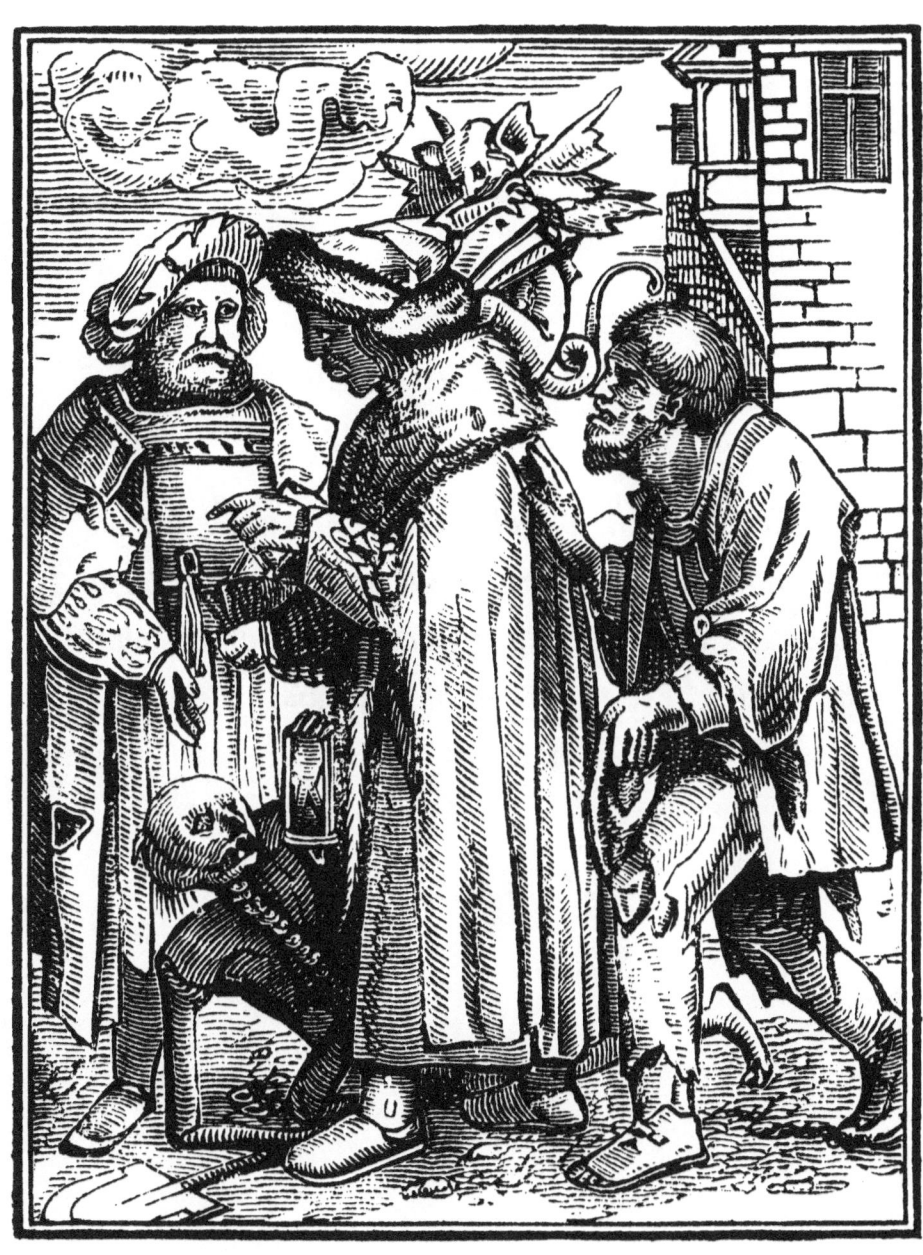

XXI.
THE PREACHER

Death with a stole about his neck stands behind the preacher, and holds a jaw-bone over his head, typifying perhaps thereby that he is the best preacher of the two.

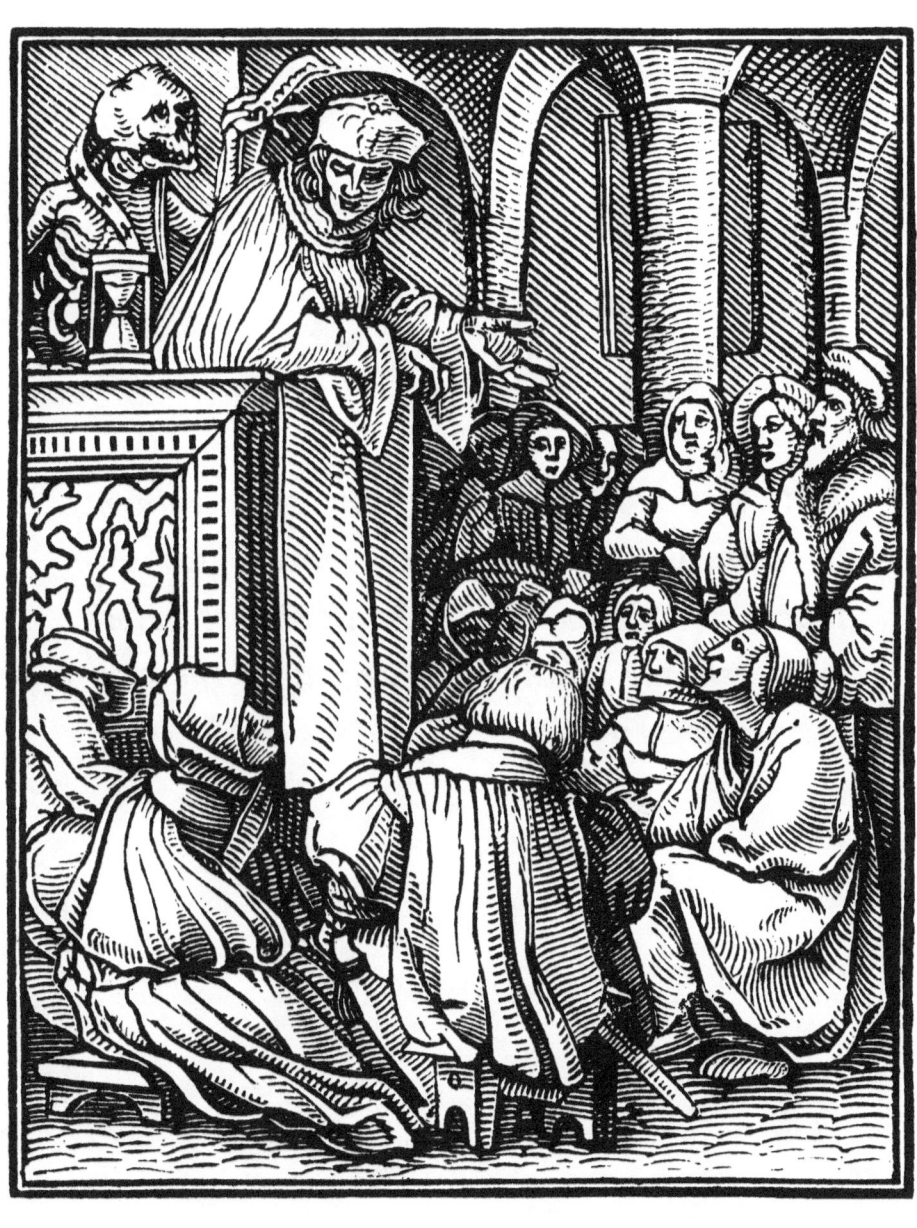

XXII.
THE PRIEST

He is carrying the viaticum, or sacrament, to some dying person. Attendants follow with tapers and holy water. Death strides before, with bell and lanthorn, to announce the coming of the priest.

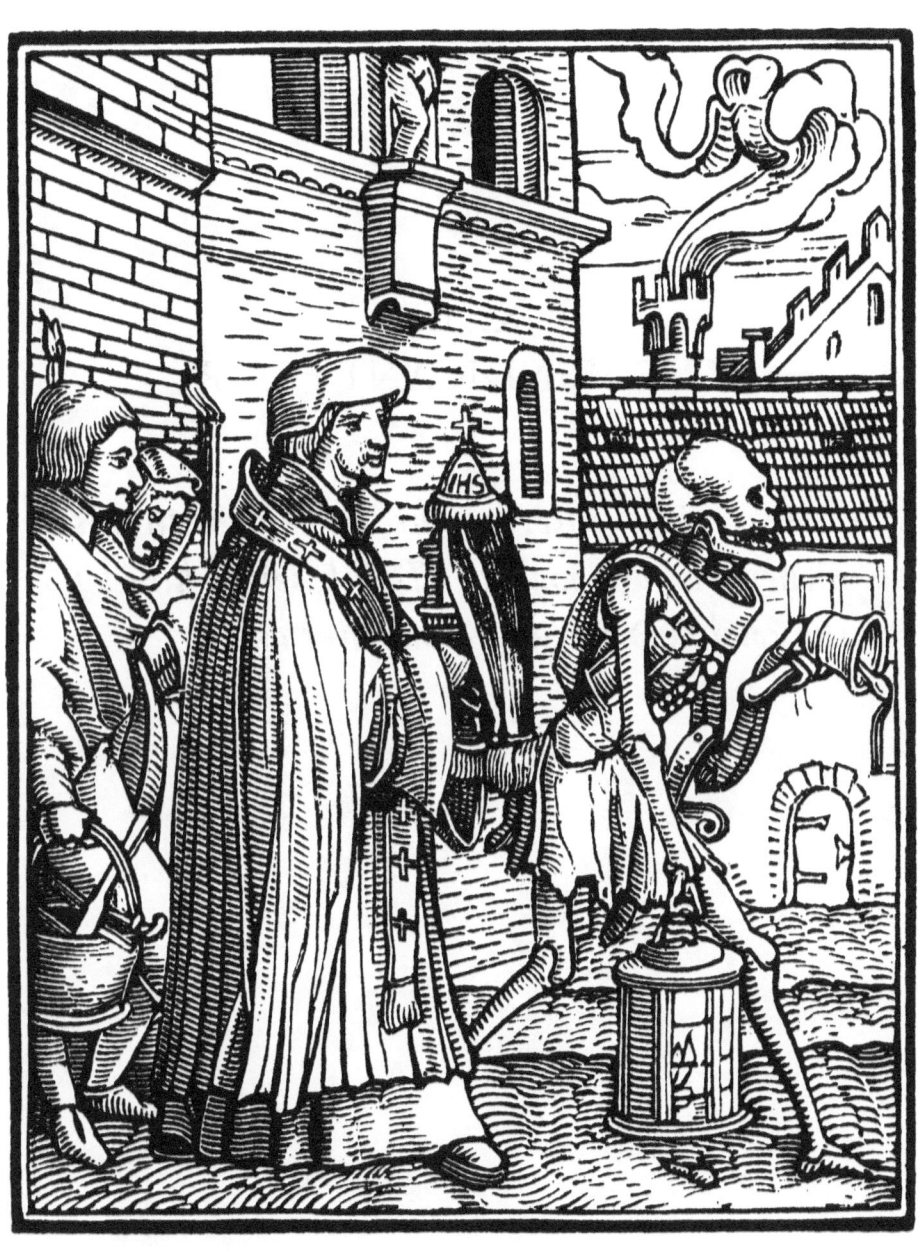

XXIII.
THE MENDICANT FRIAR

He is just entering his convent with his money-box and wallet. Death seizes him by the cowl, and forcibly drags him away.

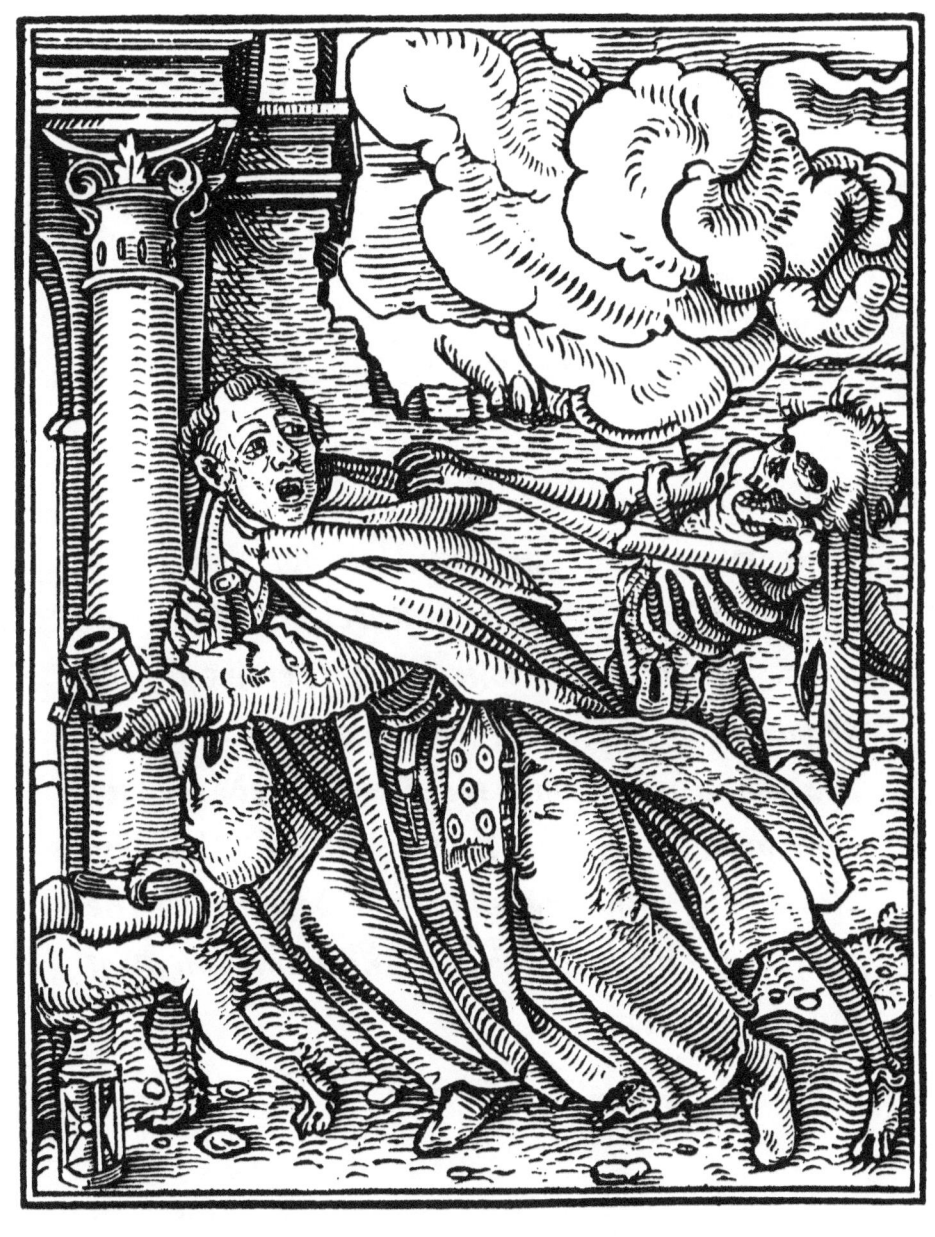

XXIV.
THE NUN

Here is a mixture of gallantry and religion. The young lady has admitted her lover into her apartment. She is kneeling before an altar, and hesitates whether to persist in her devotions or listen to the amorous music of the young man, who, seated on a bed, touches a theorbo lute. Death extinguished the candles on the altar, by which the designer of the subject probably intimates the punishment of unlawful love.

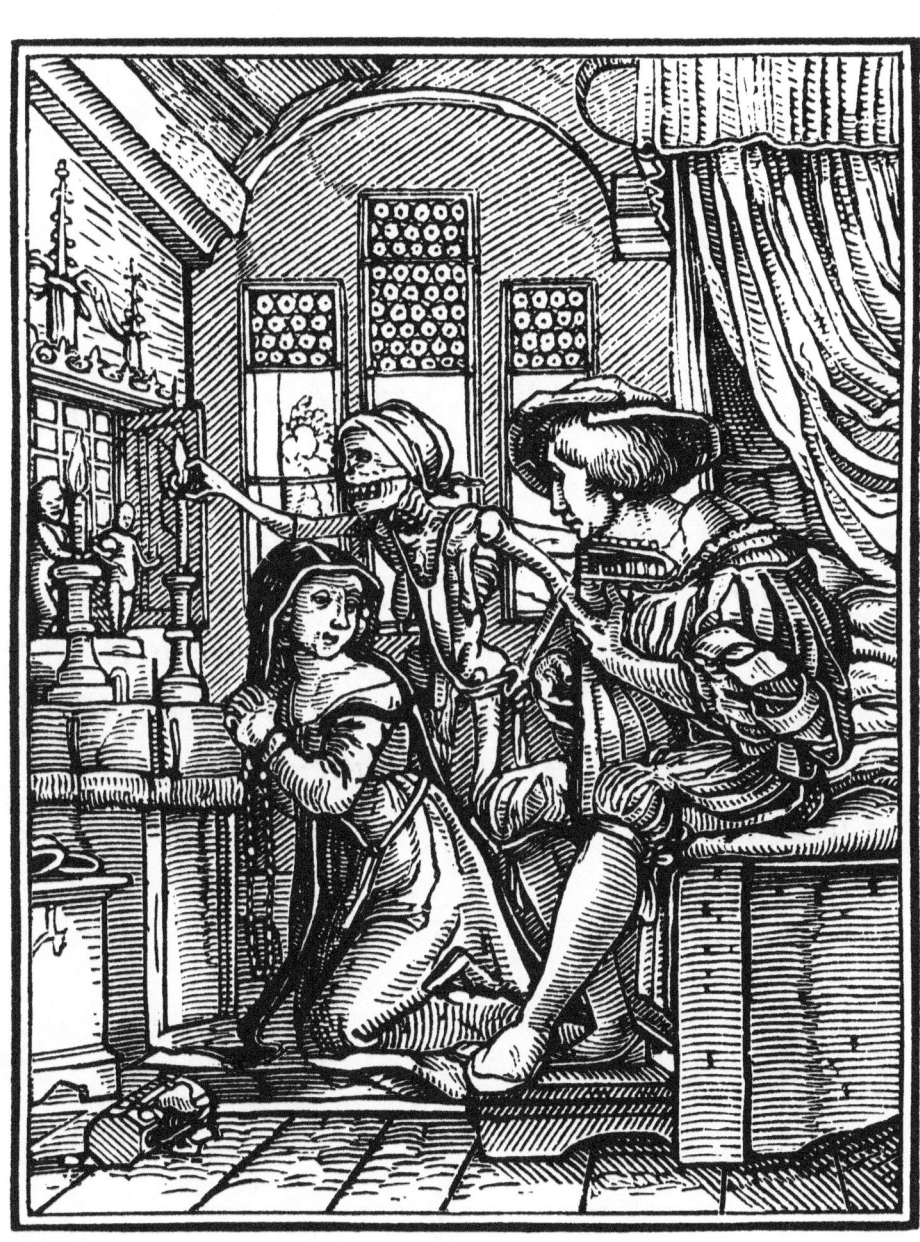

XXV.
THE OLD WOMAN

She is accompanied by two Deaths, one of whom, playing on a stickado, or wooden psalter, precedes her. She seems more attentive to her rosary of bones than to the music, whilst the other Death impatiently urges her forward with blows.

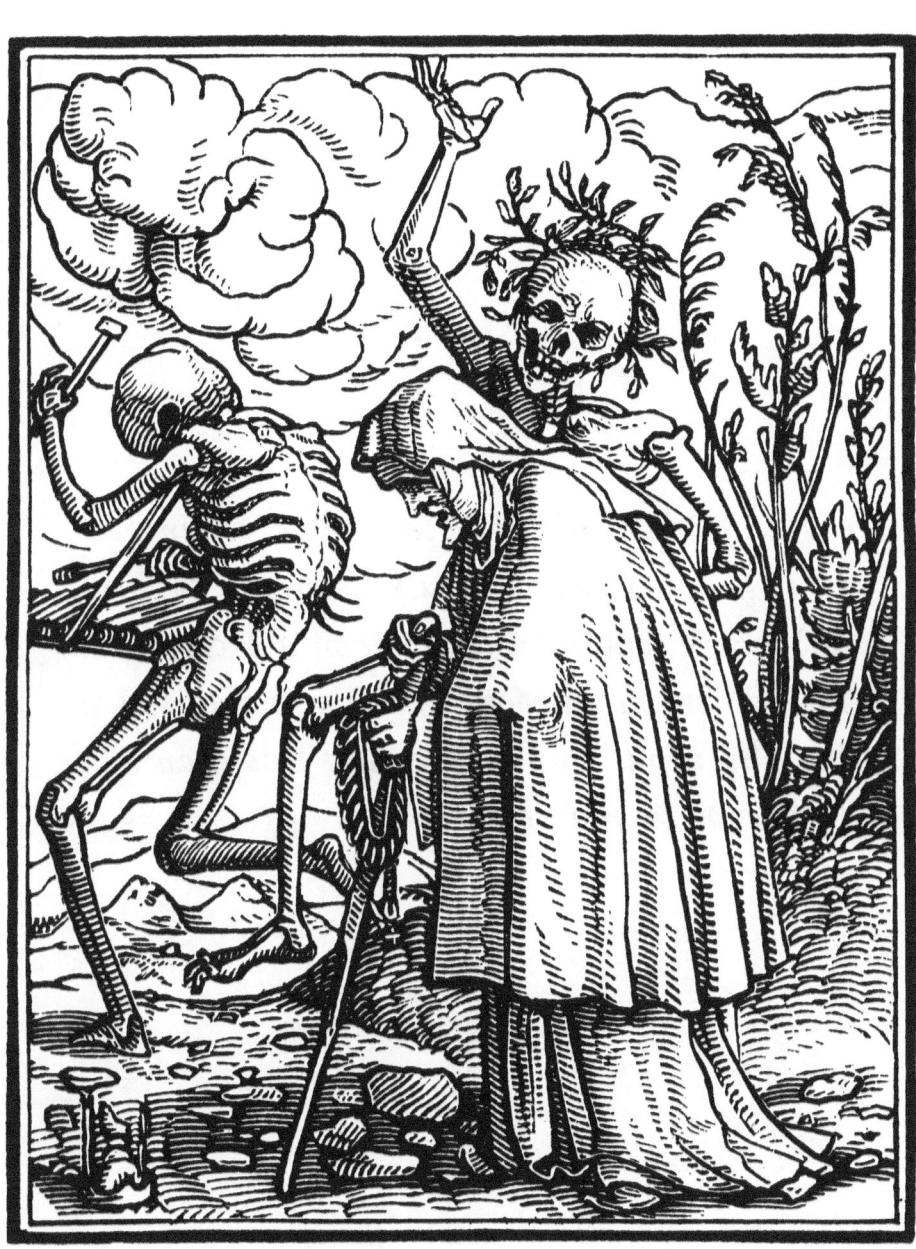

XXVI.
THE PHYSICIAN

He holds out his hand to receive, for inspection, a urinal which death presents to him, and which contains the water of a decrepit old man whom he introduces, and seems to say to the physician "Canst thou cure this man who is already in my power?"

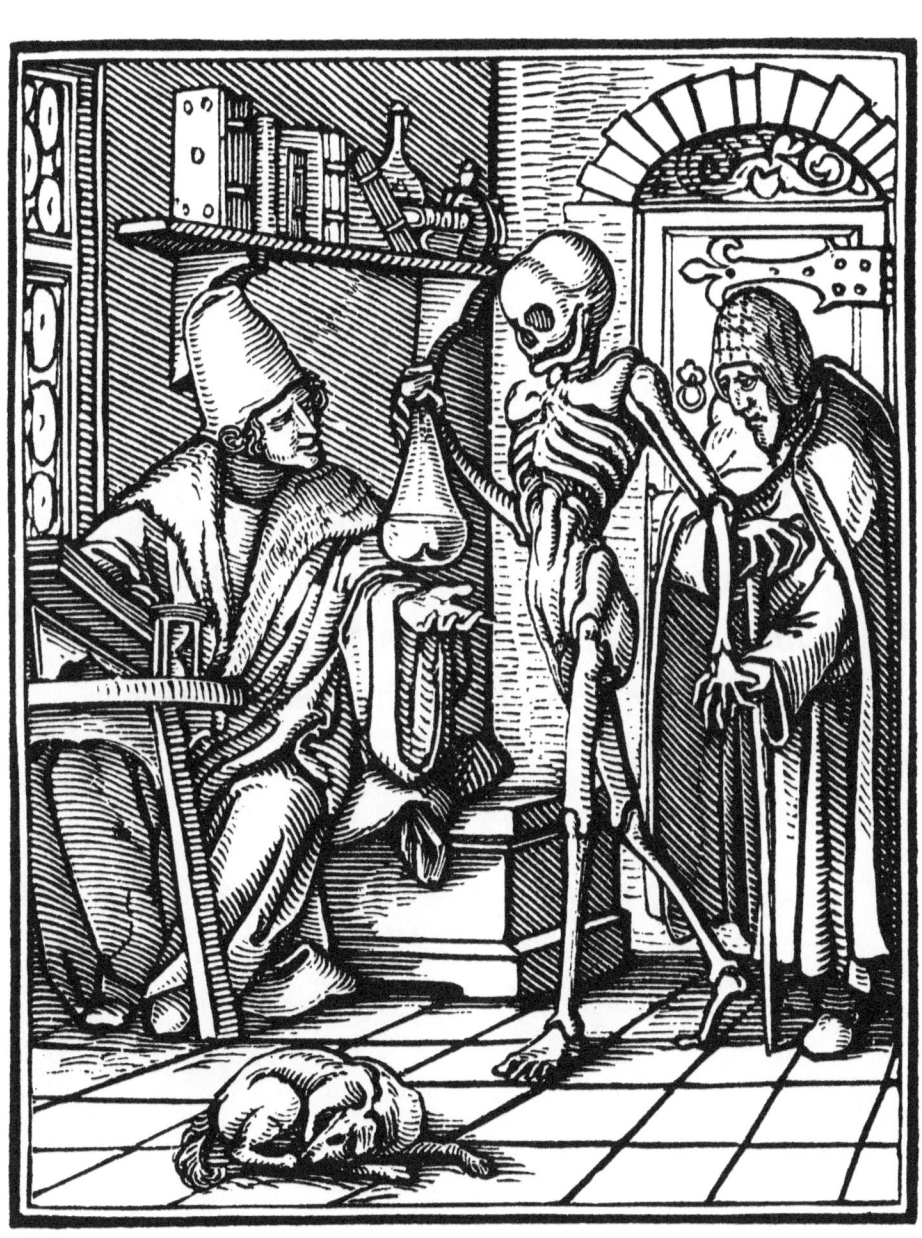

XXVII.
THE ASTROLOGER

He is seen in his study, looking attentively at a suspended sphere. Death holds out a skull to him, and seems, in mockery, to say, "Here is a better subject for your contemplation."

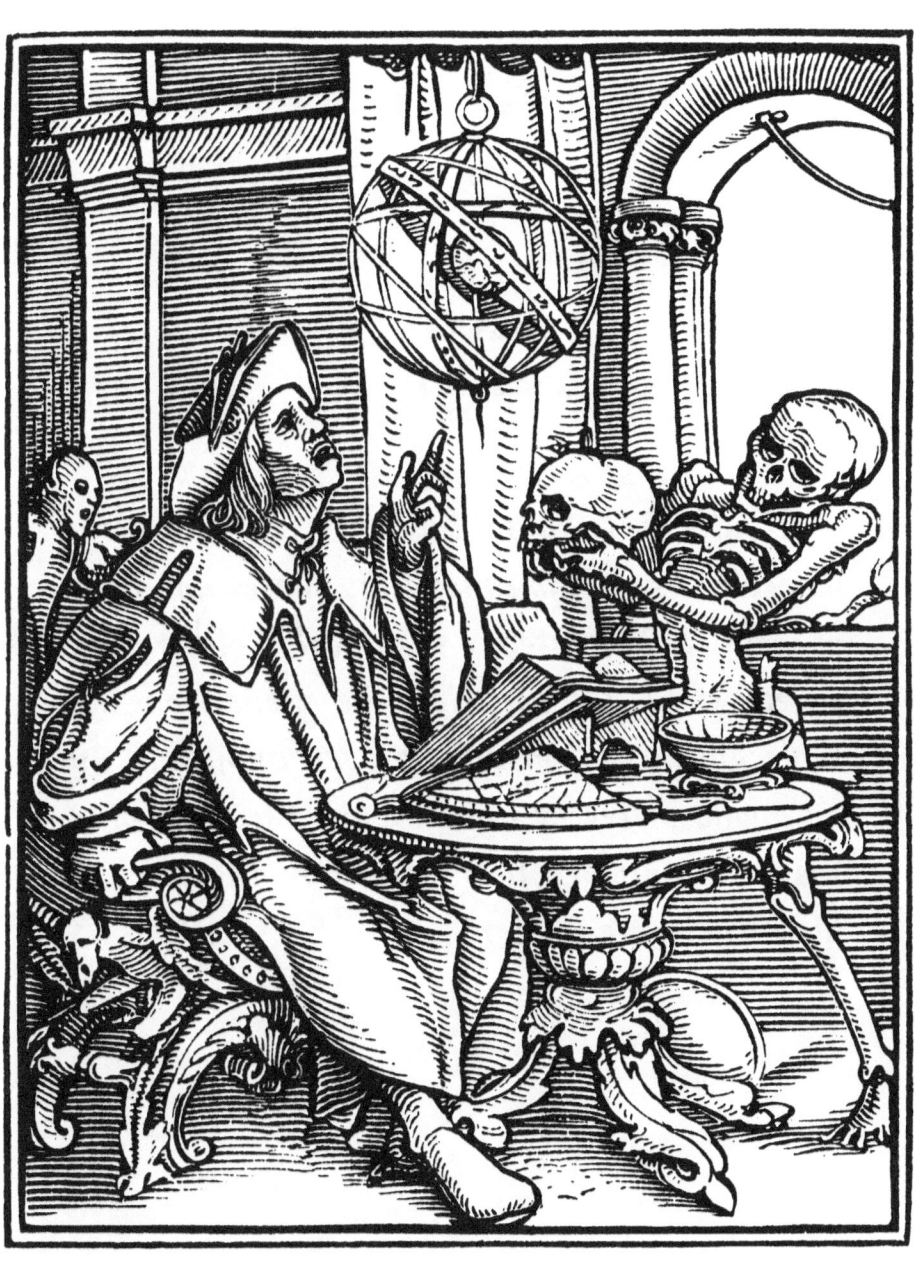

XXVIII.
THE MISER

Death has burst into his strong room, where he is sitting among his chests and bags of gold, and, seated on a stool, deliberately collects into a large dish the money on the table which the miser had been counting. In an agony of terror and despair, the poor man seems to implore forbearance on the part of his unwelcome visitor.

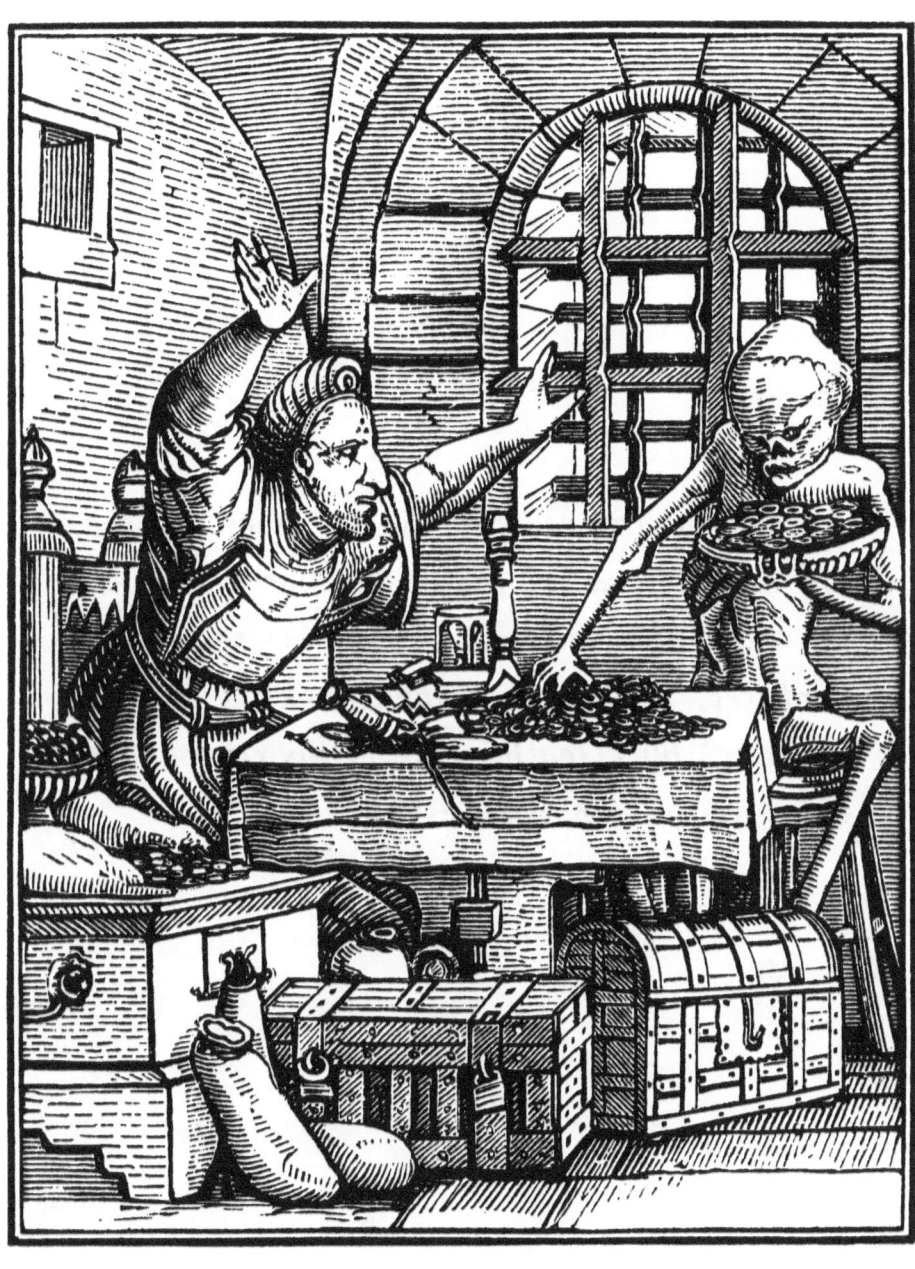

XXIX.
THE MERCHANT

After having escaped the perils of the sea, and happily reached the wished-for shore with his bales of merchandize; this too secure adventurer, whilst contemplating his riches, is surprised by Death. One of his companions holds up his hands in despair.

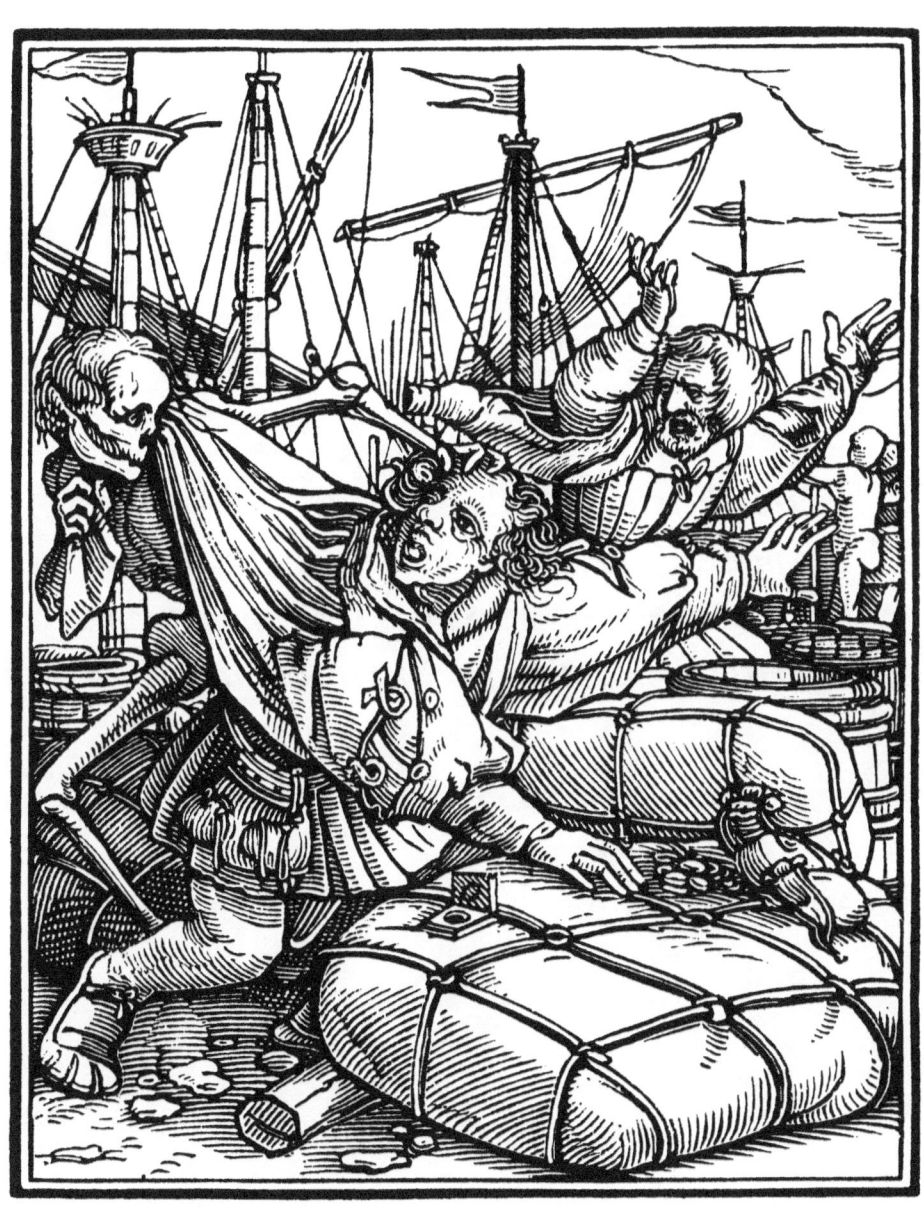

XXX.
THE SHIP IN A TEMPEST

Death is vigorously employed in breaking the mast. The owner of the vessel is wringing his hands in despair. One man seems perfectly resigned to his impending fate.

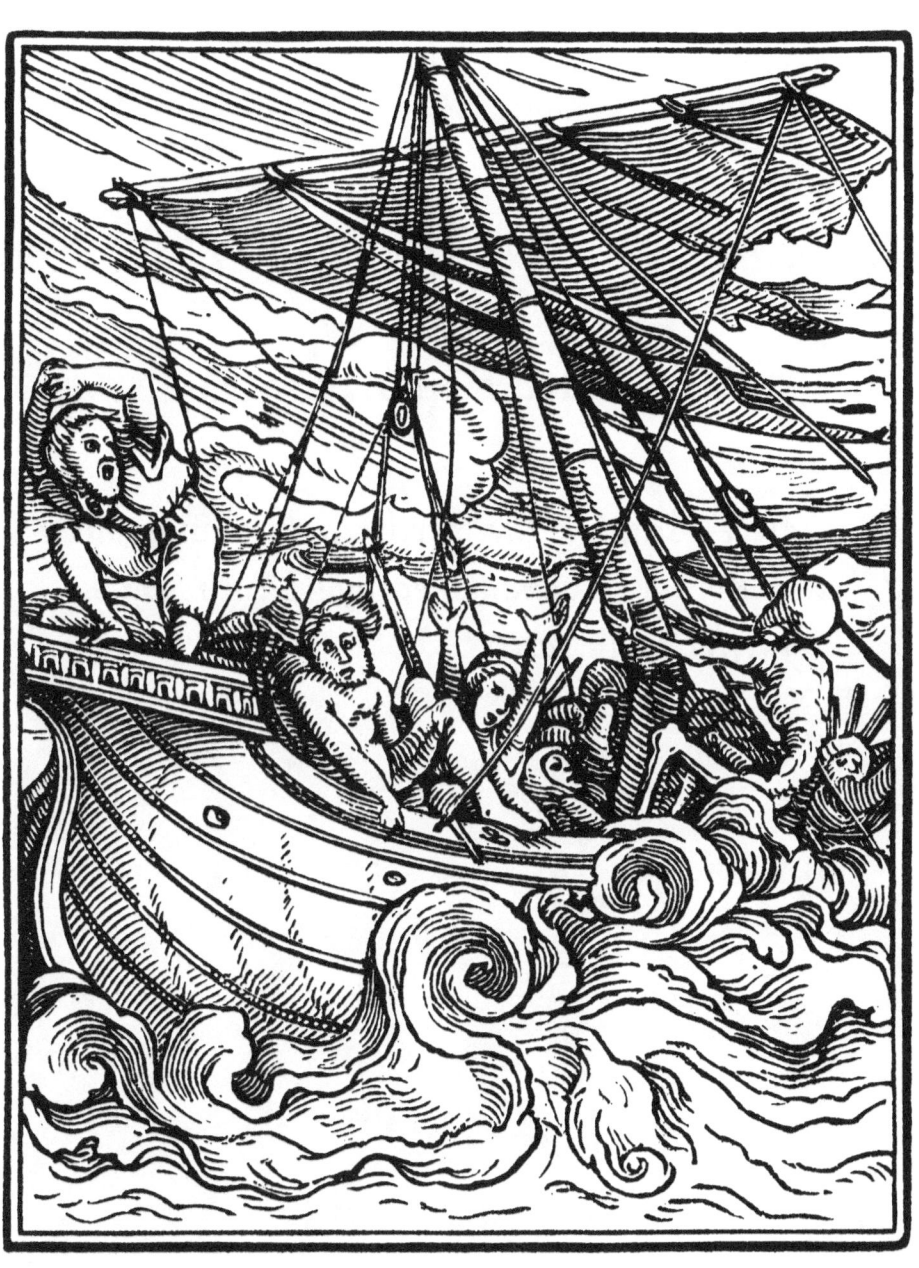

XXXI.
THE KNIGHT

After escaping the perils in his numerous combats, he is vanquished by Death, whom he ineffectually resists.

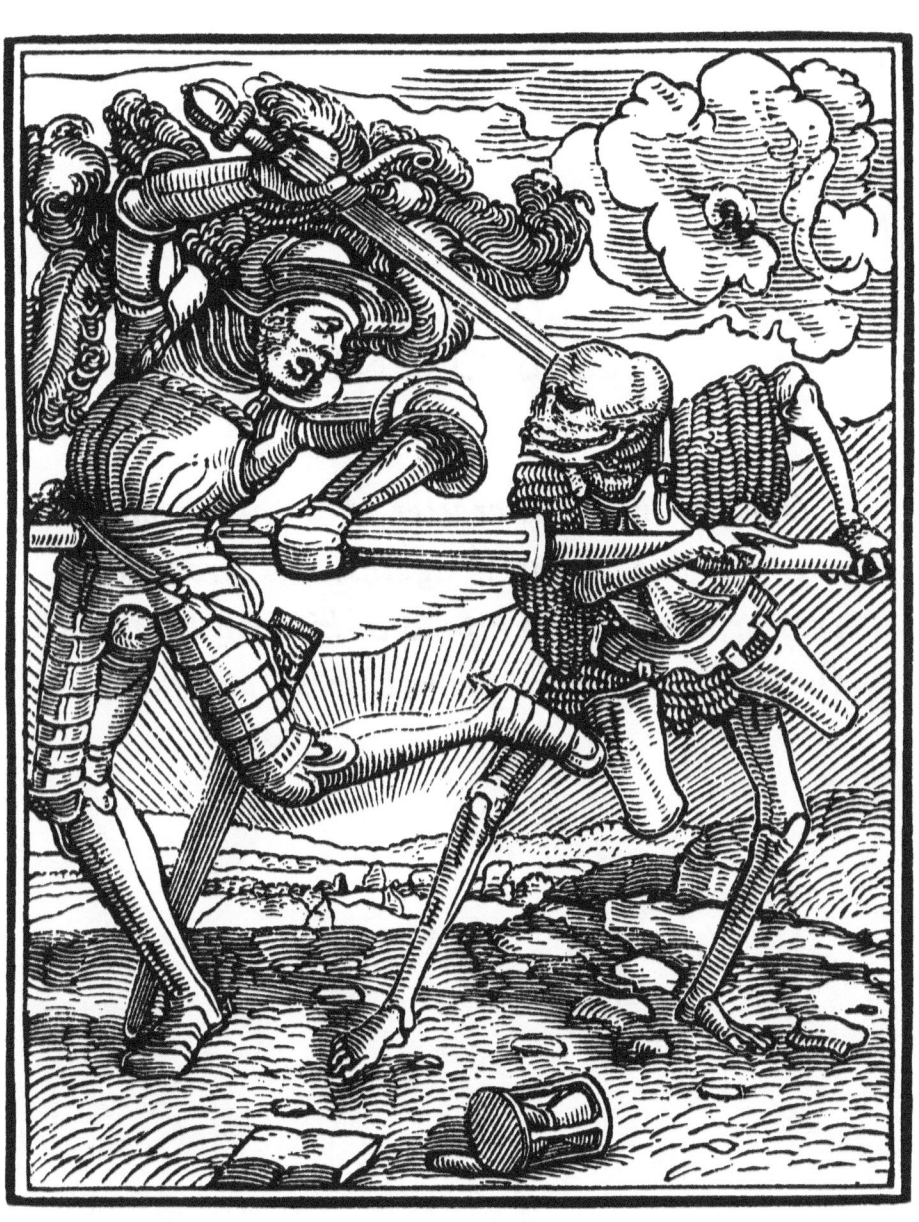

XXXII.
THE COUNT

Death, in the character of a ragged peasant, revenges himself against his proud oppressor by crushing him with his own armour. On the ground lie a helmet, crest, and flail.

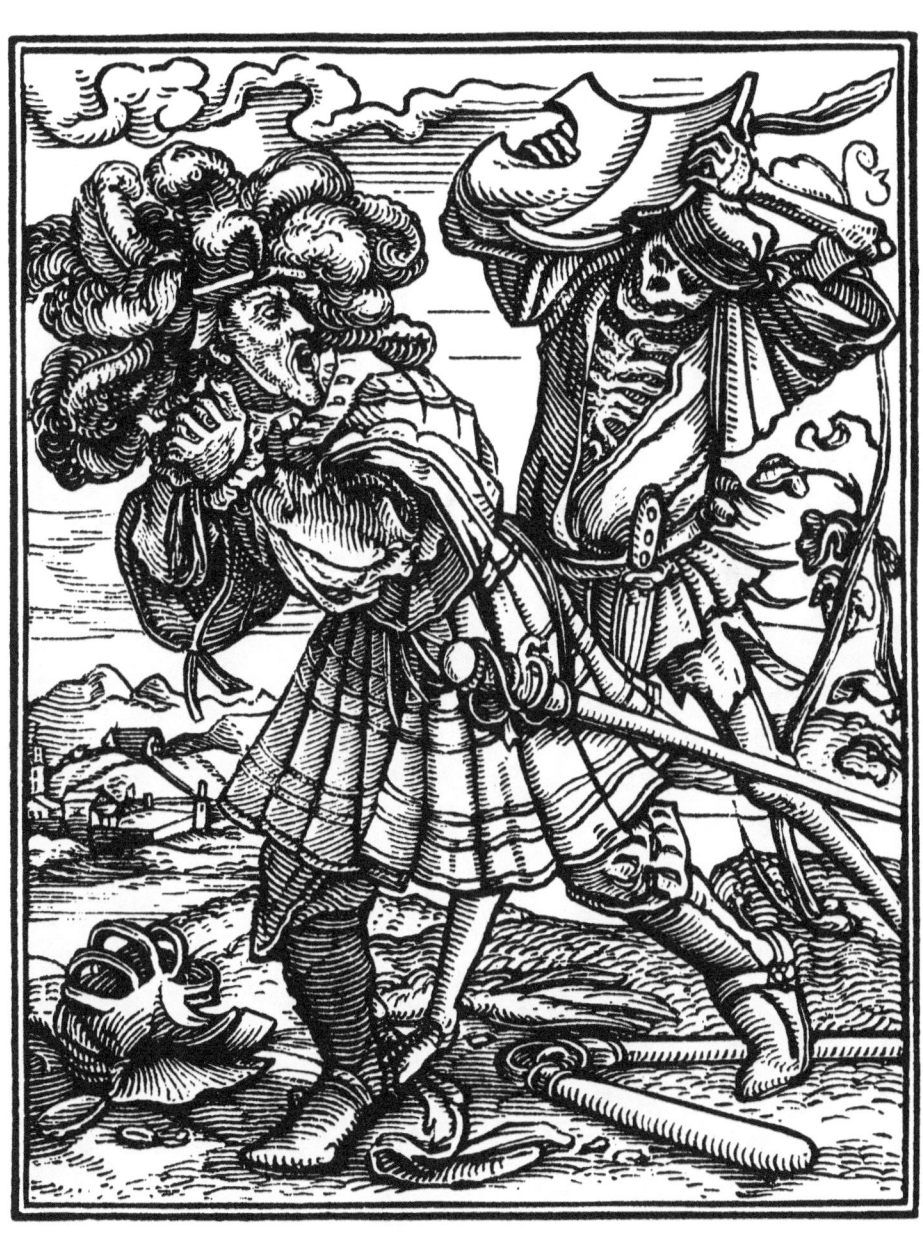

XXXIII.
THE OLD MAN

*Death leads his aged victim to the grave,
beguiling him with the music of a dulcimer.*

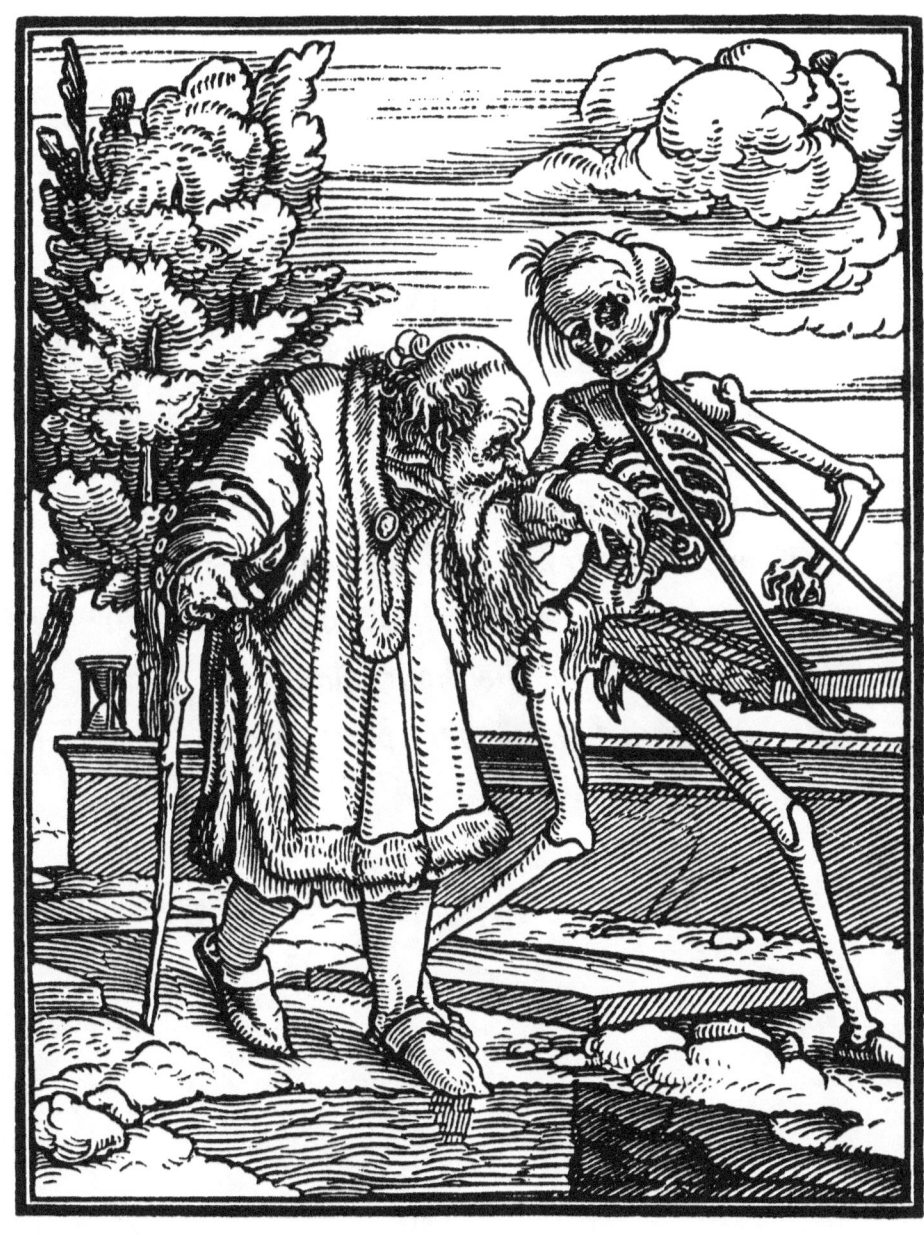

XXXIV.
THE COUNTESS

She receives from an attendant the splendid dress and ornaments with which she is about to equip herself. On a chest are seen a mirror, a brush, and the hour-glass of Death, who, standing behind her, places on her neck a collar of bones.

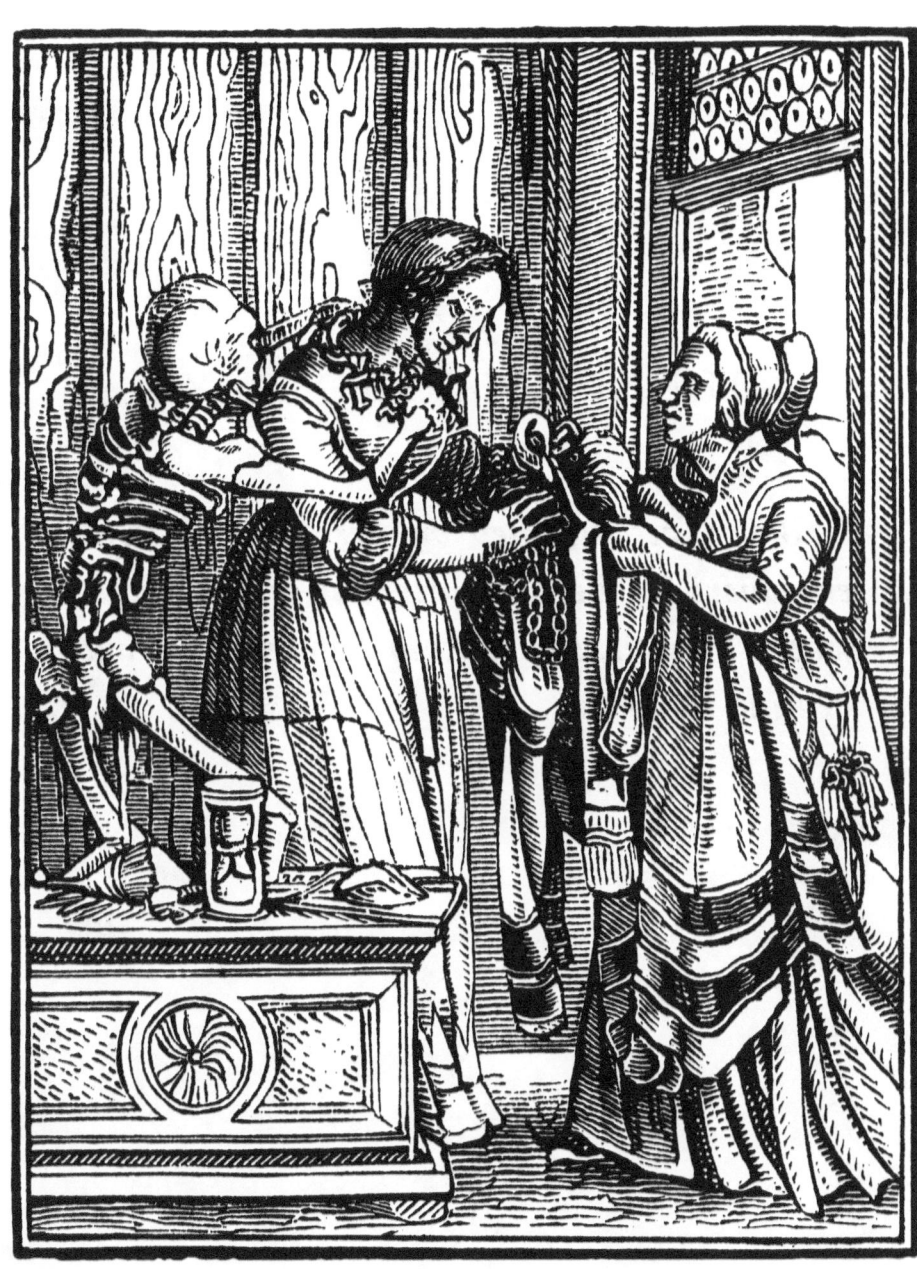

XXXV.
THE NEW-MARRIED LADY

She is accompanied by her husband, who endeavors to divert her attention from Death, who is insidiously dancing before them and beating tambour.

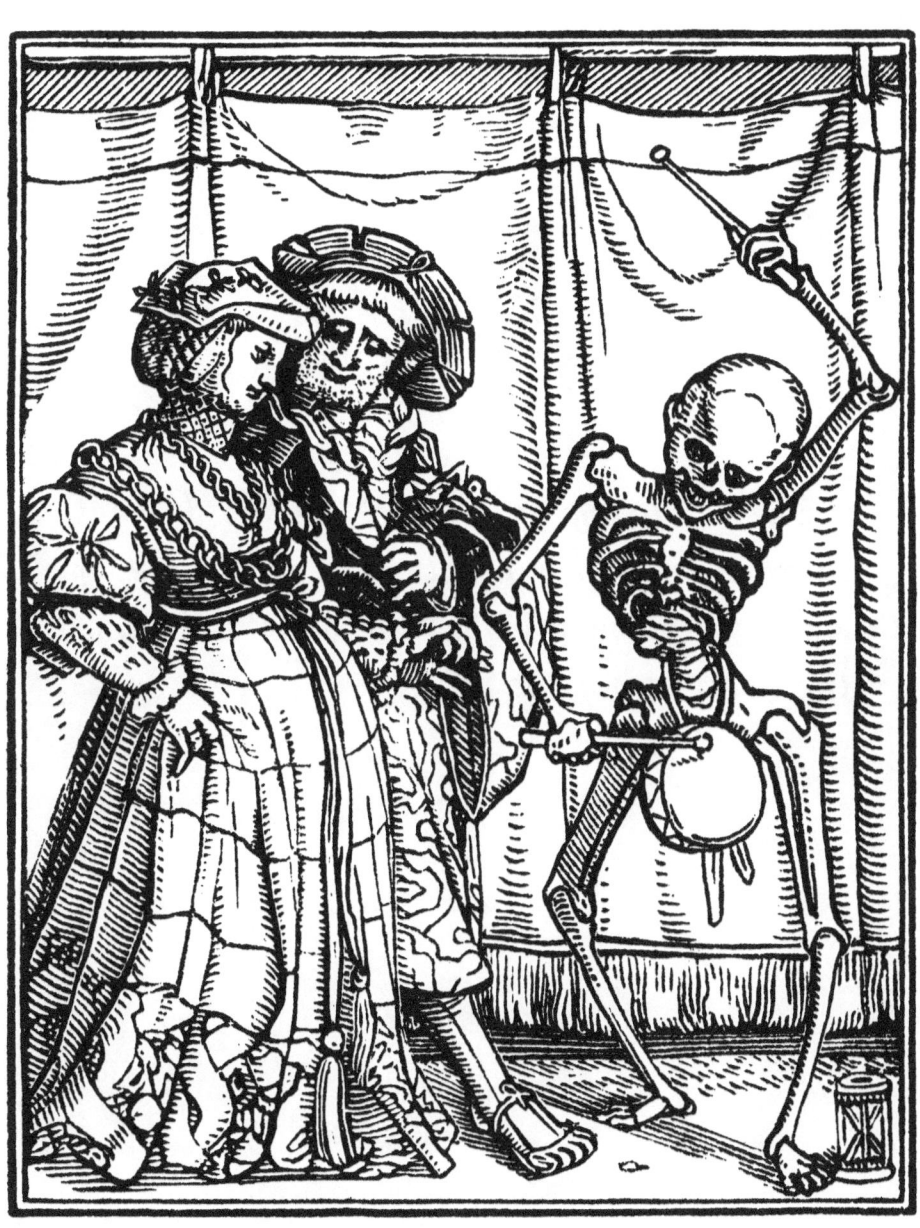

XXXVI.
THE DUCHESS

She is sitting up, dressed, in her bed, at the foot of which are two Deaths, one of whom plays on a violin, the other is pulling the clothes from the bed.

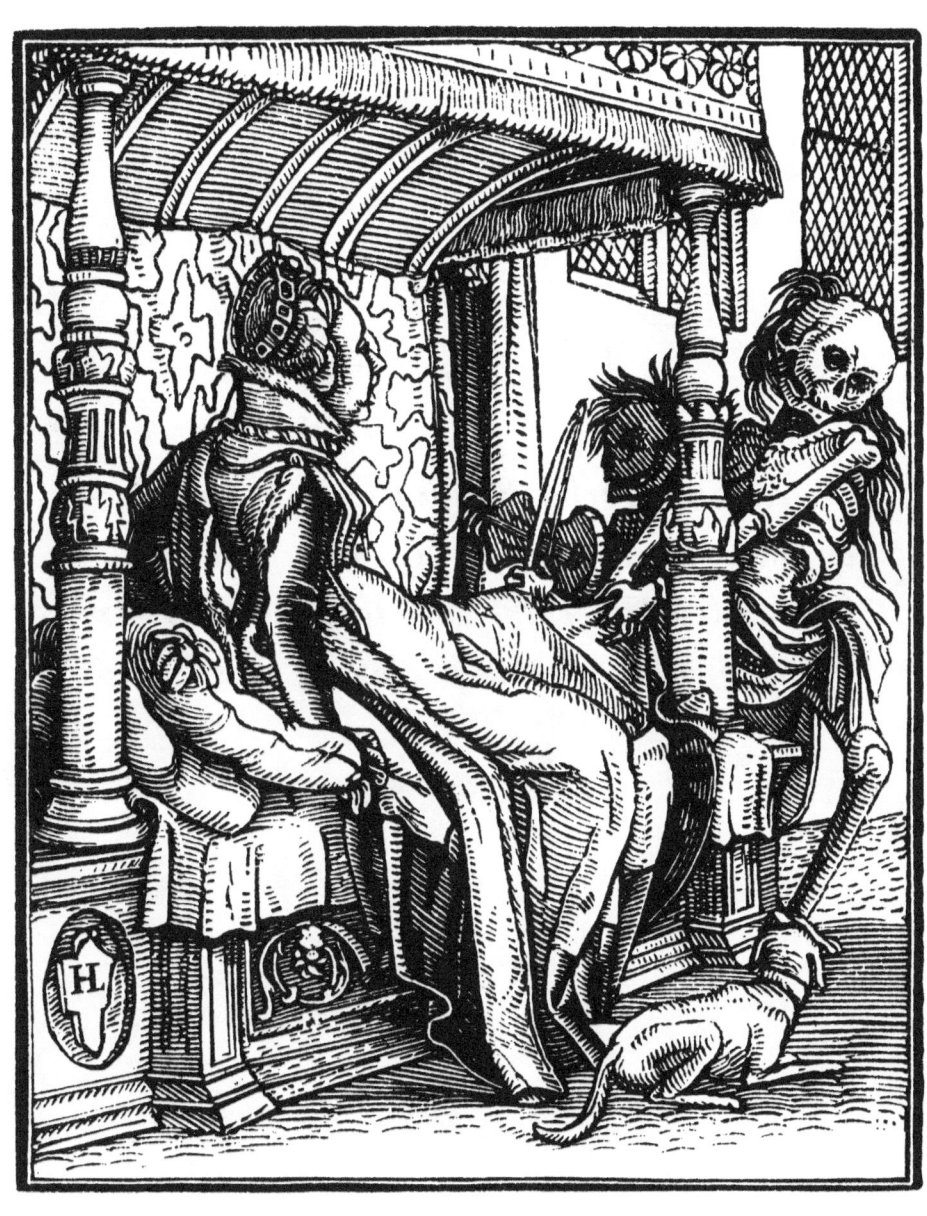

XXXVII.
THE PEDDLER

Accompanied by his dog, and heavily laden, he is proceeding on his way, when he is intercepted by death, who forcibly pulls him back. Another Death is playing on a trump-marine.

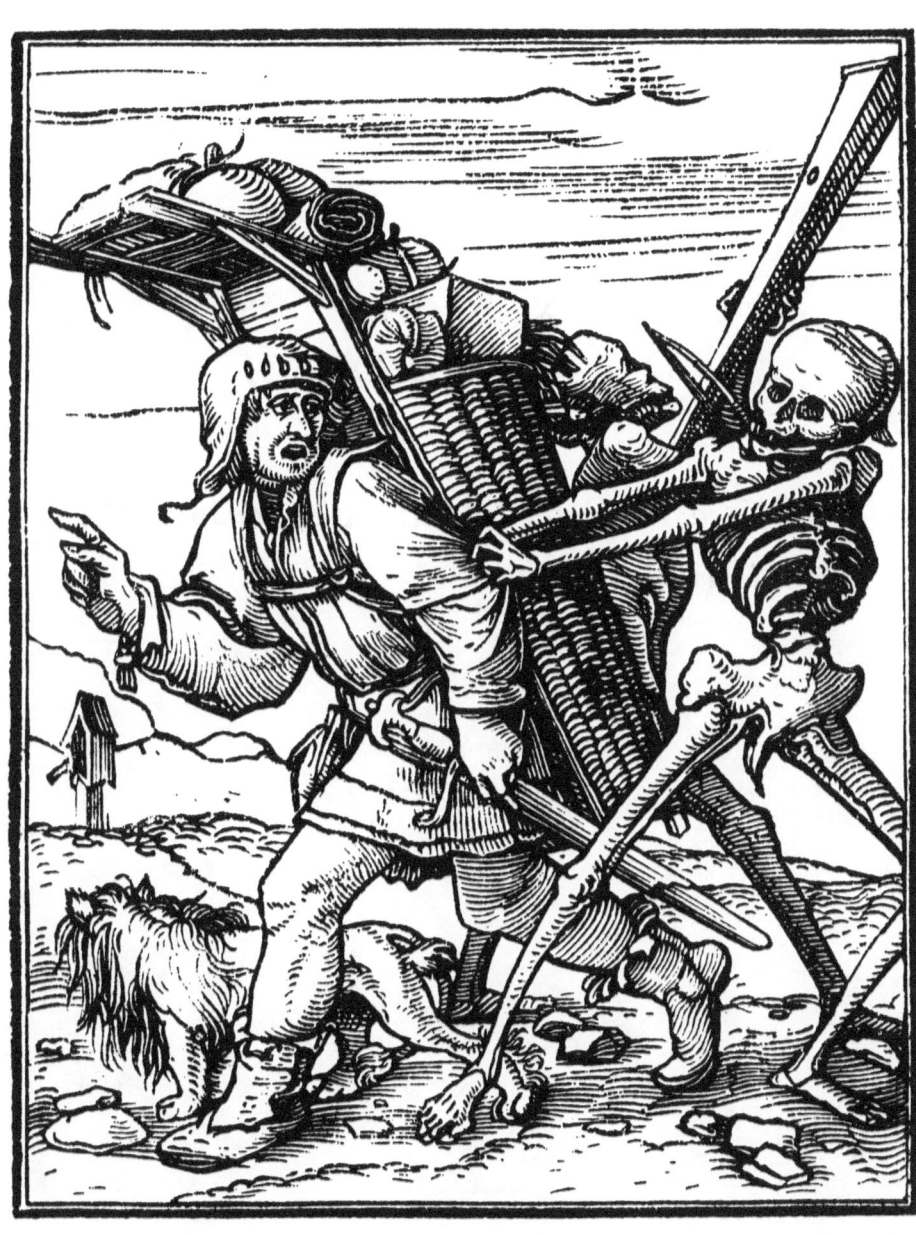

XXXVIII.
THE HUSBANDMAN

He is assisted by Death, who conducts the horses of his plough.

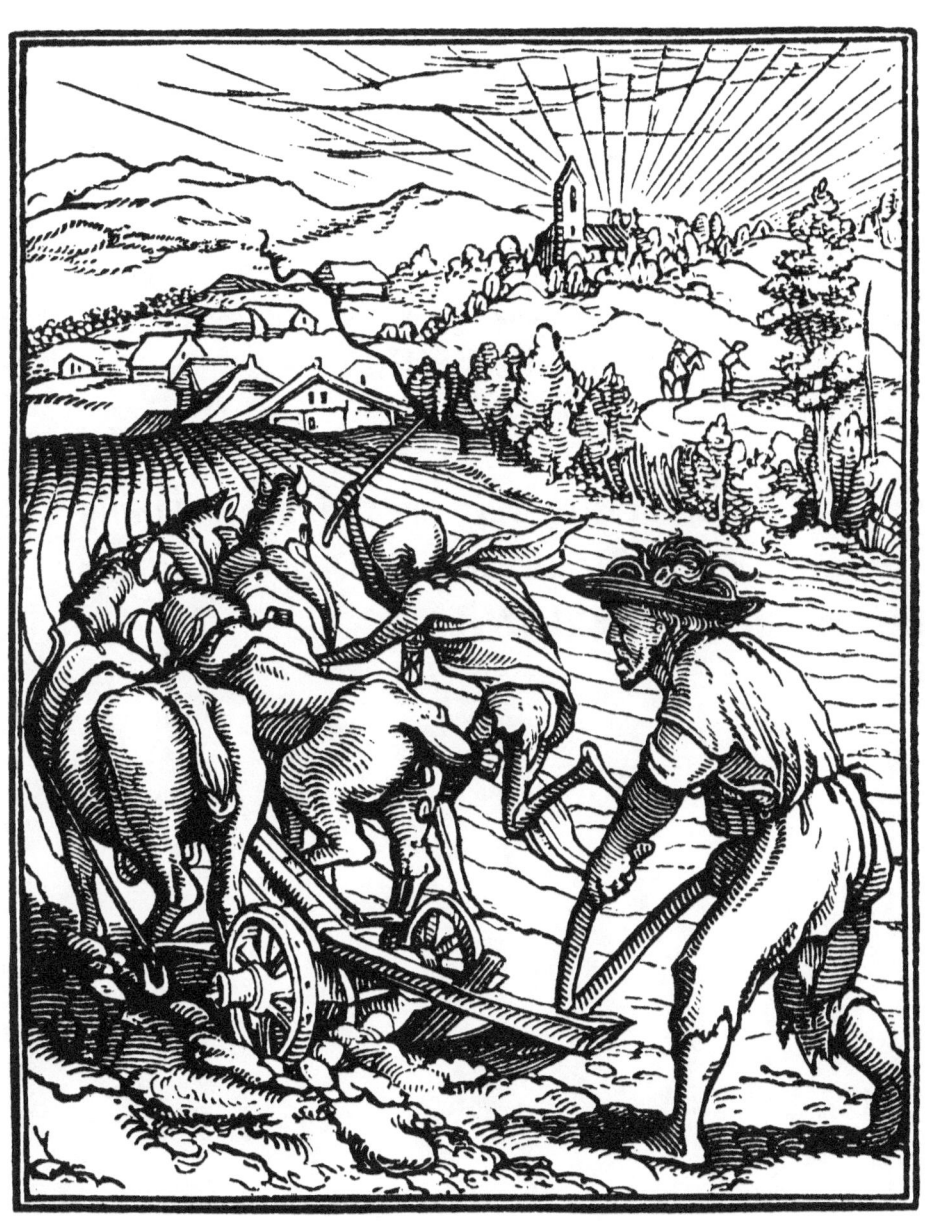

XXXIV.
THE CHILD

A female cottager is preparing her family mess, when Death enters and carries off the youngest of her children.

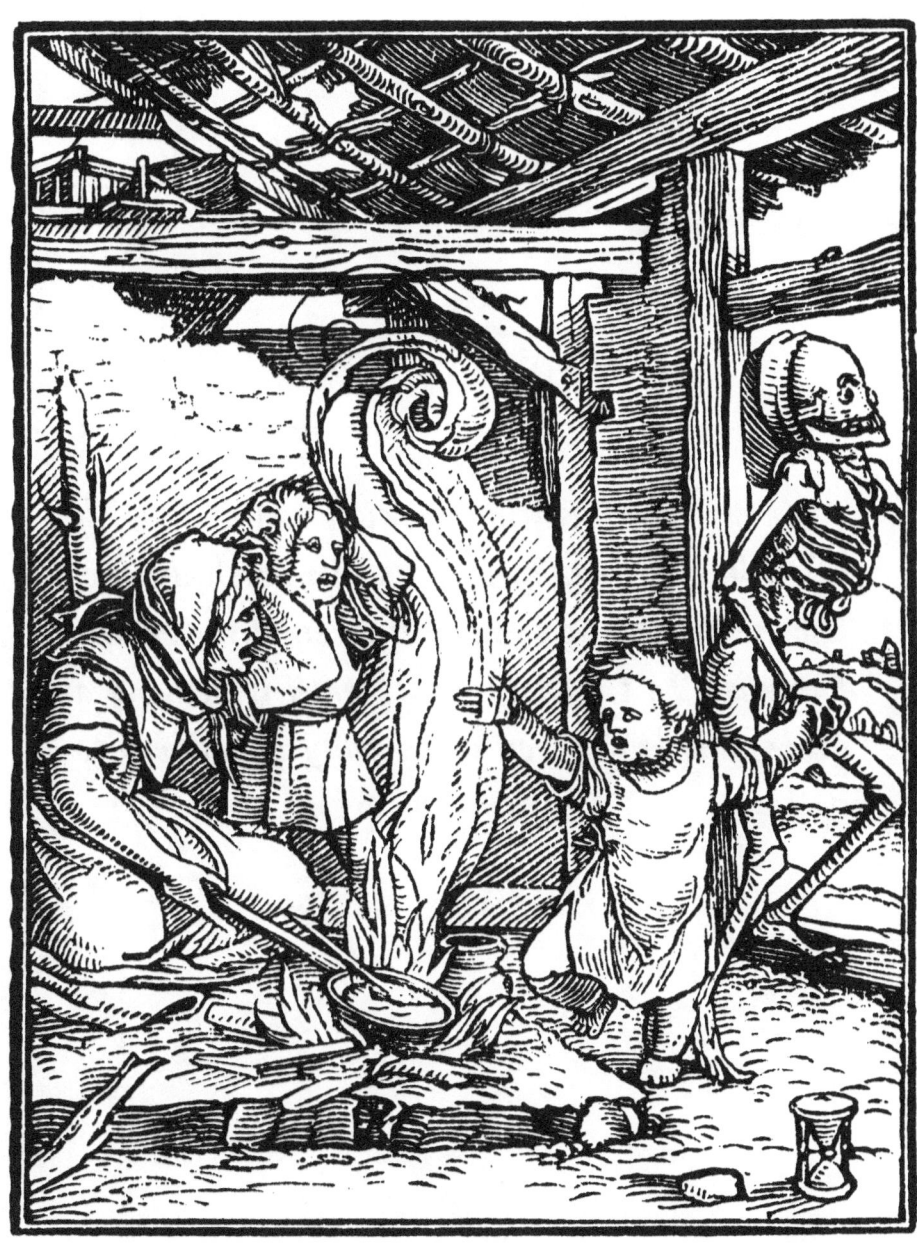

XL.
THE SOLDIER

He is engaged in unequal combat with
Death, who simply attacks him with a bone.
On the ground lie some of his demolished companions. In the distance, Death is beating a
drum, and leading on a company of soldiers to
battle.

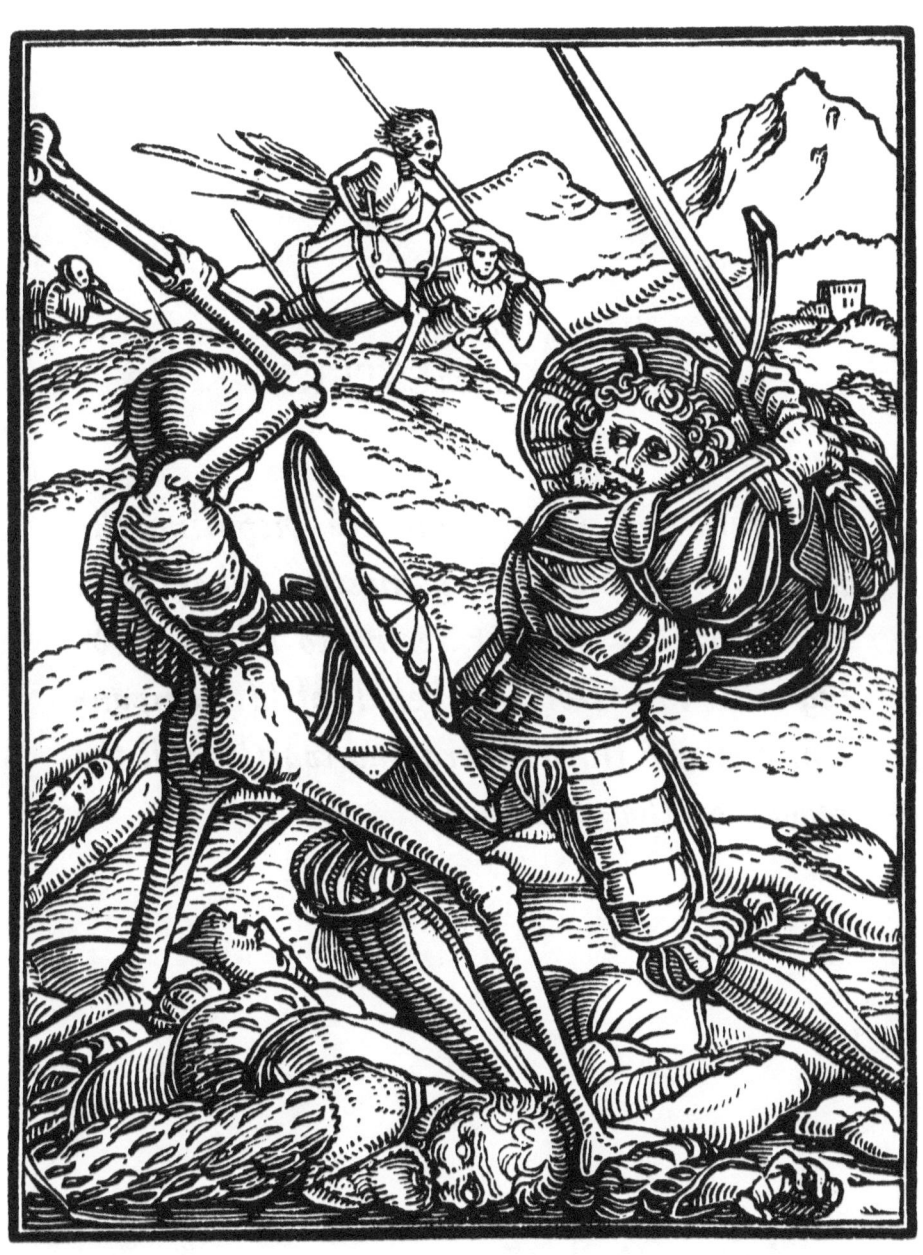

XLI.
THE GAMESTERS

Death and the Devil are disputing the possession of one of the gamesters, whom both have seized. Another seems to be interceding with the Devil on behalf of his companion, whilst a third is scraping together all the money on the table.

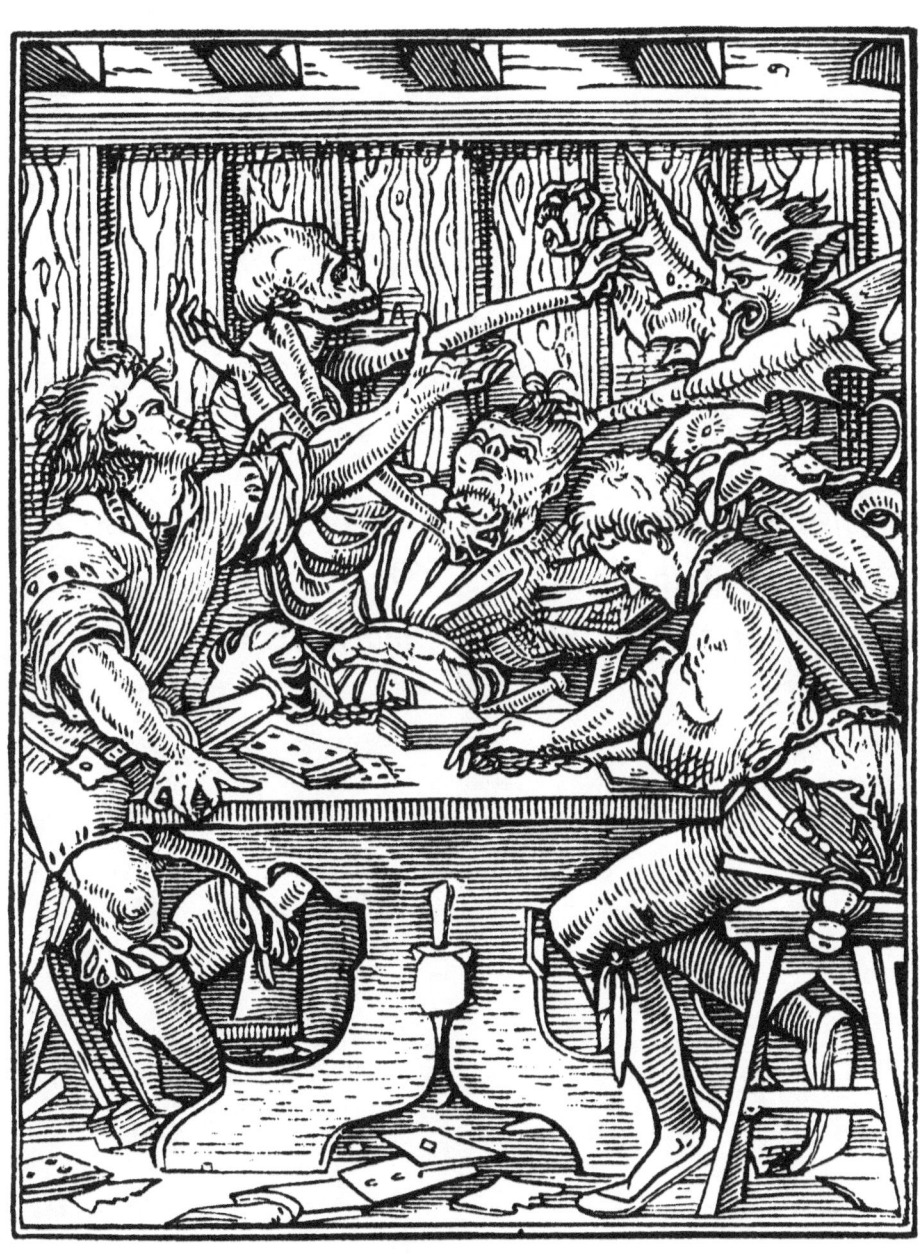

XLII.
THE DRUNKARDS

They are assembled in a brothel, and in-
temperately feasting. Death pours liquor
from a flagon into the mouth of one of the
party.

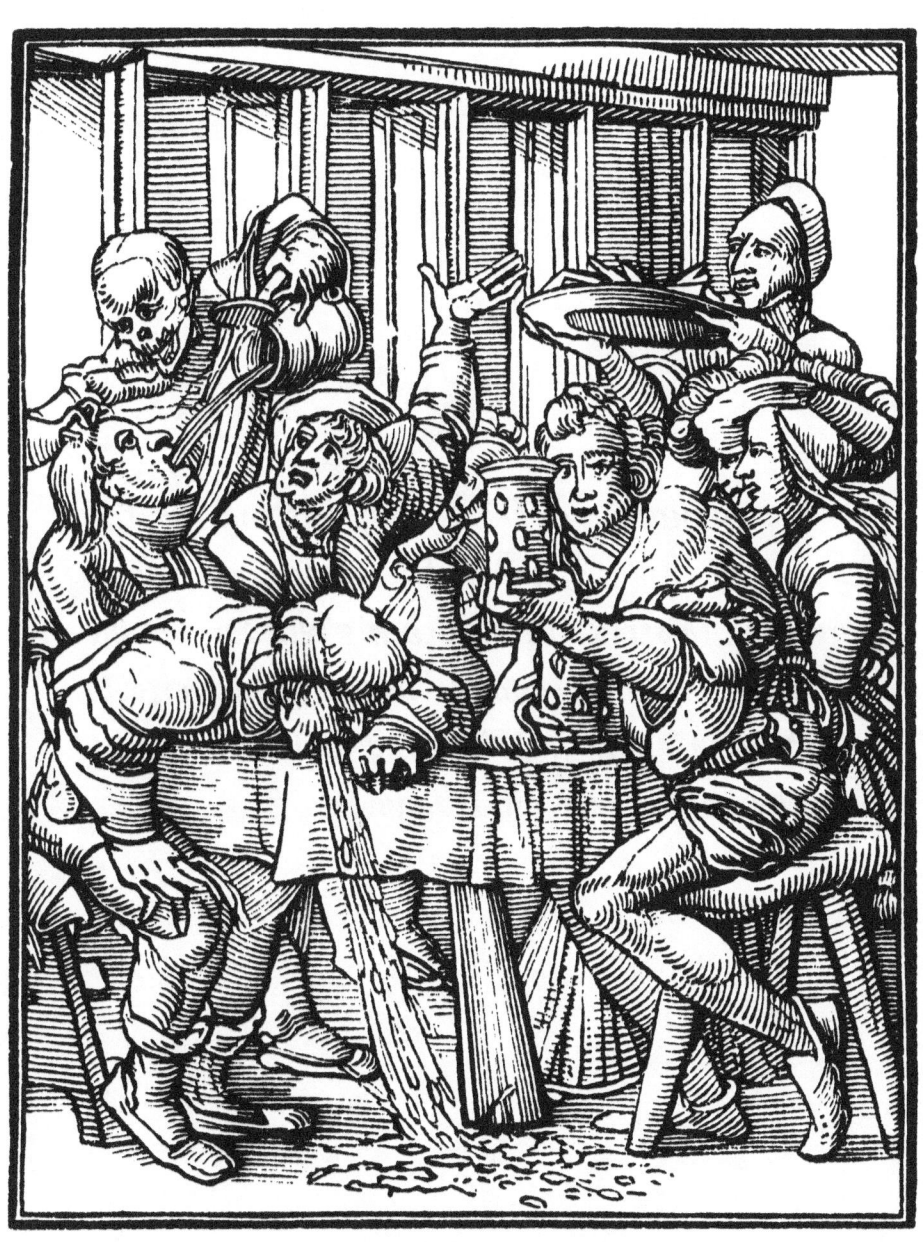

XLIII.
THE IDIOT FOOL

He is mocking Death, by putting his finger in his mouth, and at the same time endeavouring to strike him with his bladder-bauble. Death smiling, and amused at his efforts, leads him away in a dancing attitude, playing at the same time on a bagpipe.

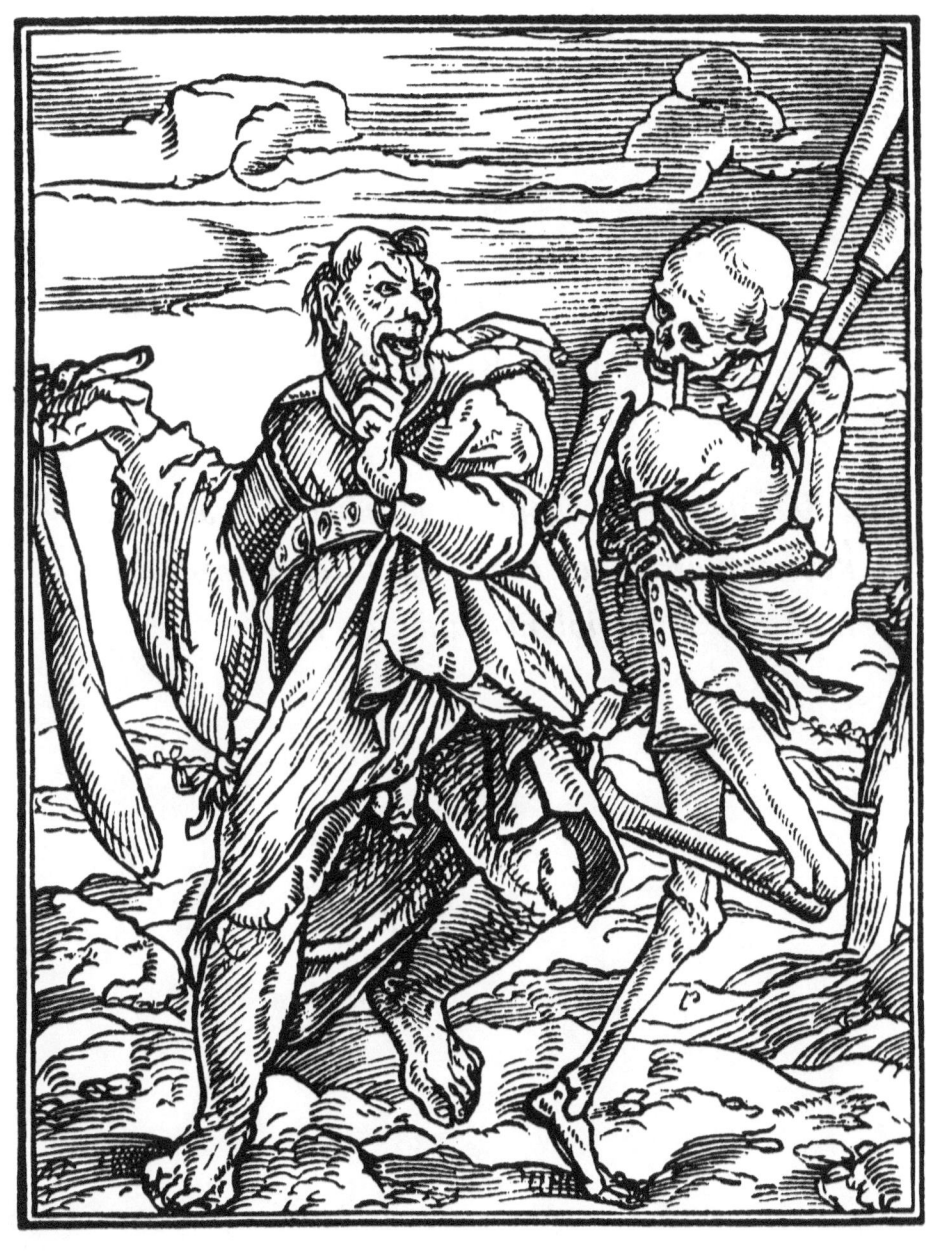

XLIV.
THE ROBBER

*Whilst he is about to plunder a poor mar-
ket-woman of her property, Death comes behind and lays violent hands on him.*

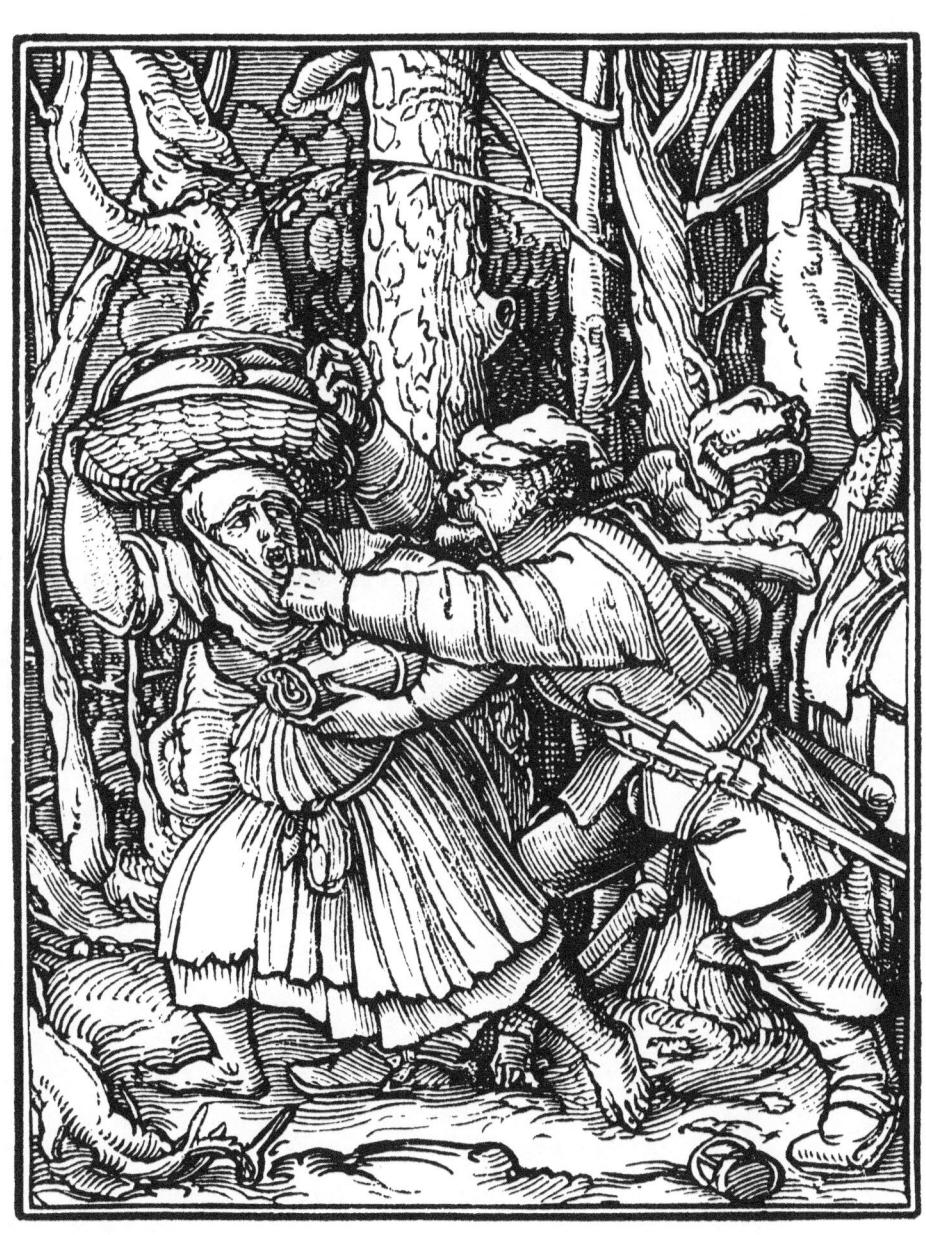

XLV.
THE BLIND MAN

Carefully measuring his steps, and uncon-scious of his perilous situation, he is led on by Death, who with one hand takes him by the cloak, both parties having hold of his staff.

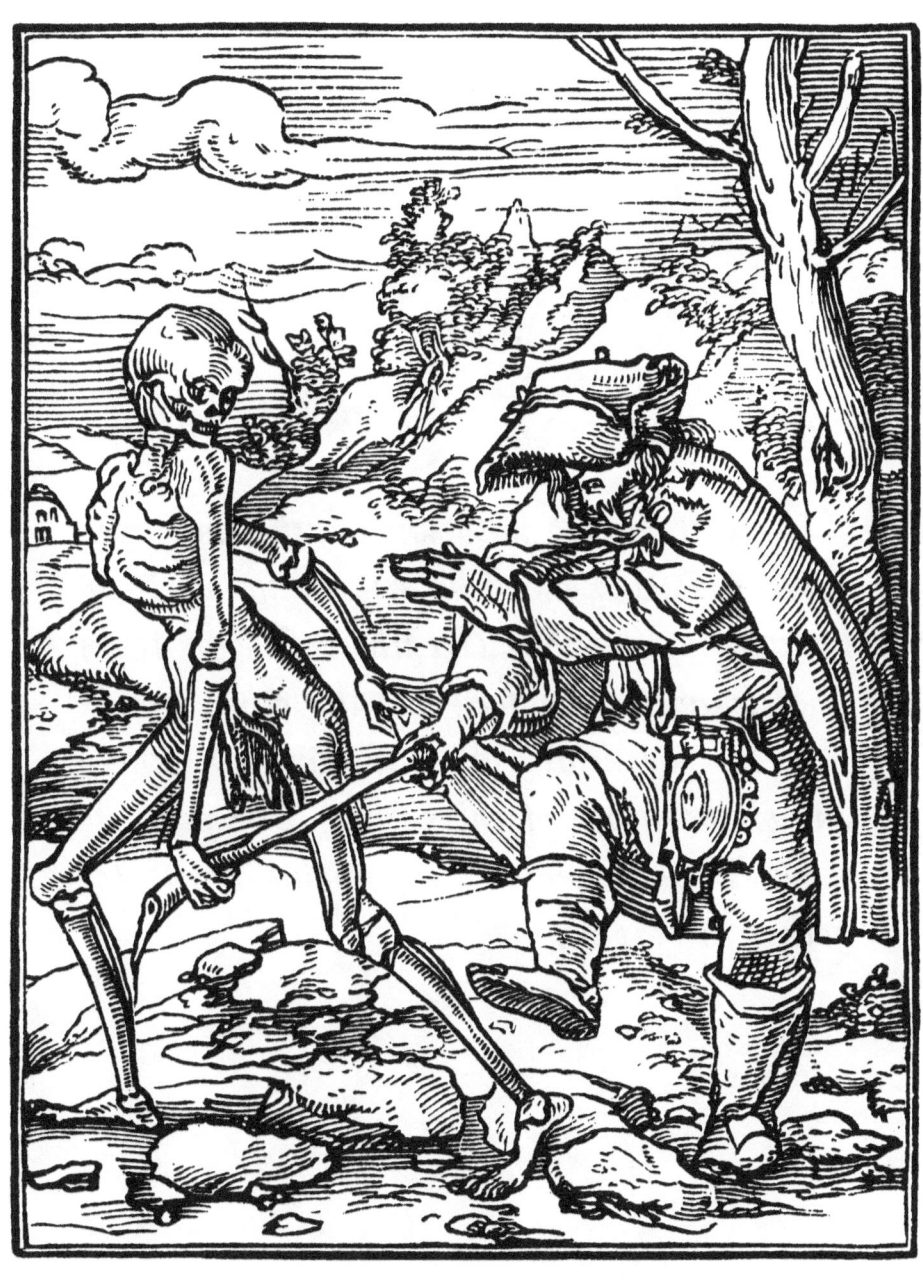

XLVI.
THE WAGGONER

His cart, loaded with wine casks, has been overturned, and one of his horses thrown down by two mischievous Deaths. One of them is carrying off a wheel, and the other is employed in wrenching off a tie that had secured one of the hoops of the casks. The poor affrighted waggoner is clasping his hands together in despair.

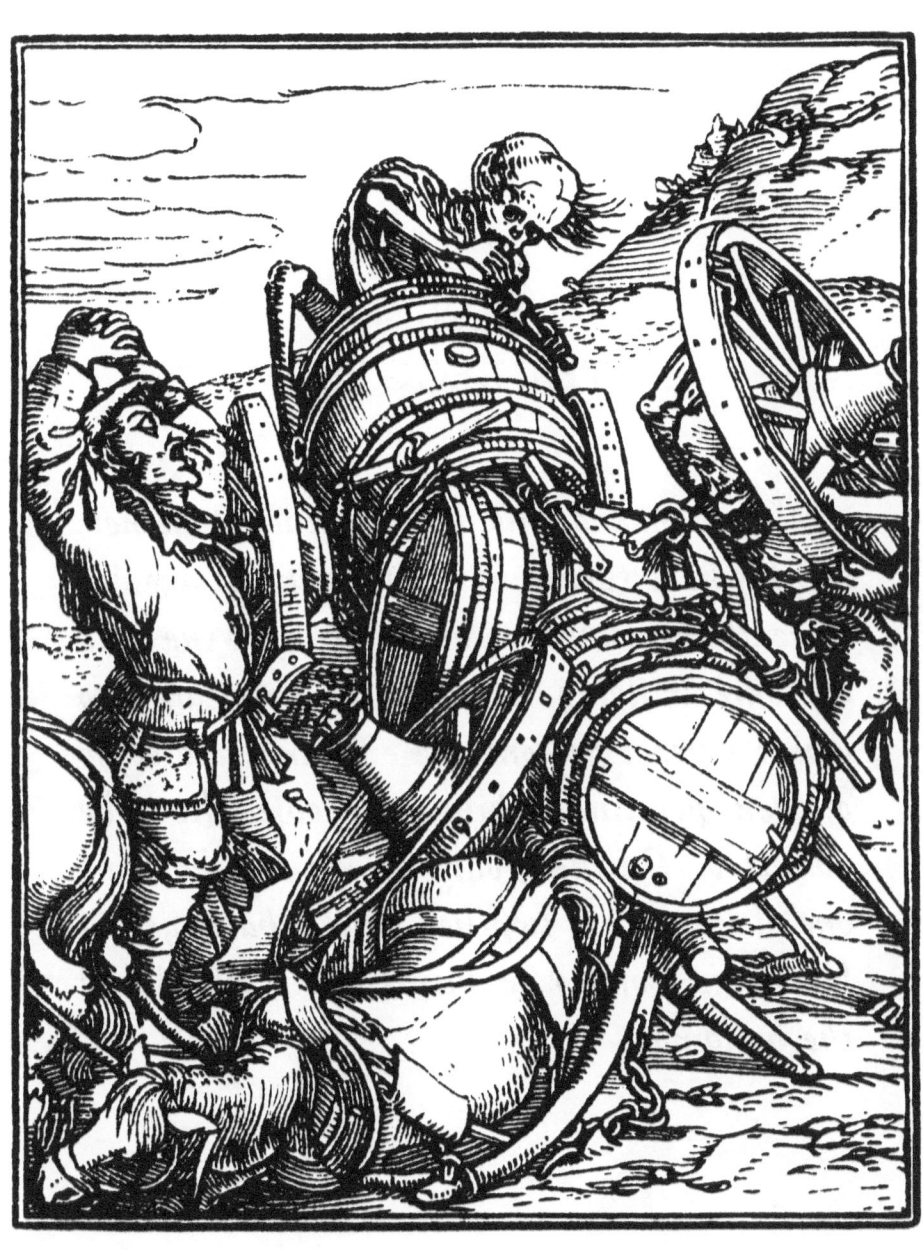

XLVII.
THE BEGGAR

Almost naked, his hands joined together, and his head turned upwards as in the agonies of death, he is sitting on straw near the gate of some building, perhaps an hospital, into which several persons are entering, and some of them pointing to him as an object fit to be admitted. On the ground lie his crutches, and one of his legs is swathed with a bandage. A female is looking on him from a window of the building.

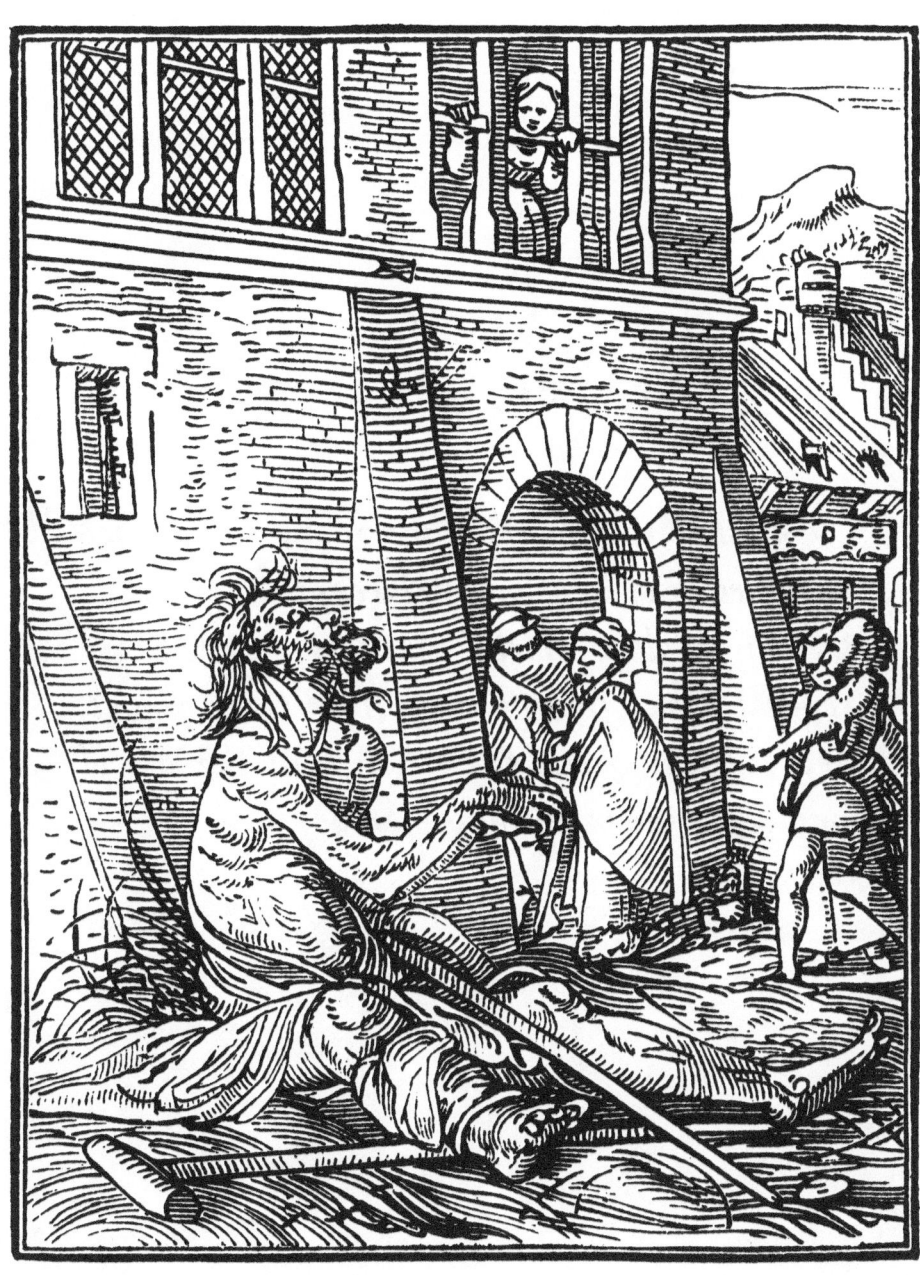

XLVIII.
THE LAST JUDGEMENT

Christ sitting on a rainbow, and surrounded by a group of angels, patriarchs, etc. rests his feet on a globe of the universe. Below are several naked figures risen from their graves, and stretching out their hands in the act of imploring judgment and mercy.

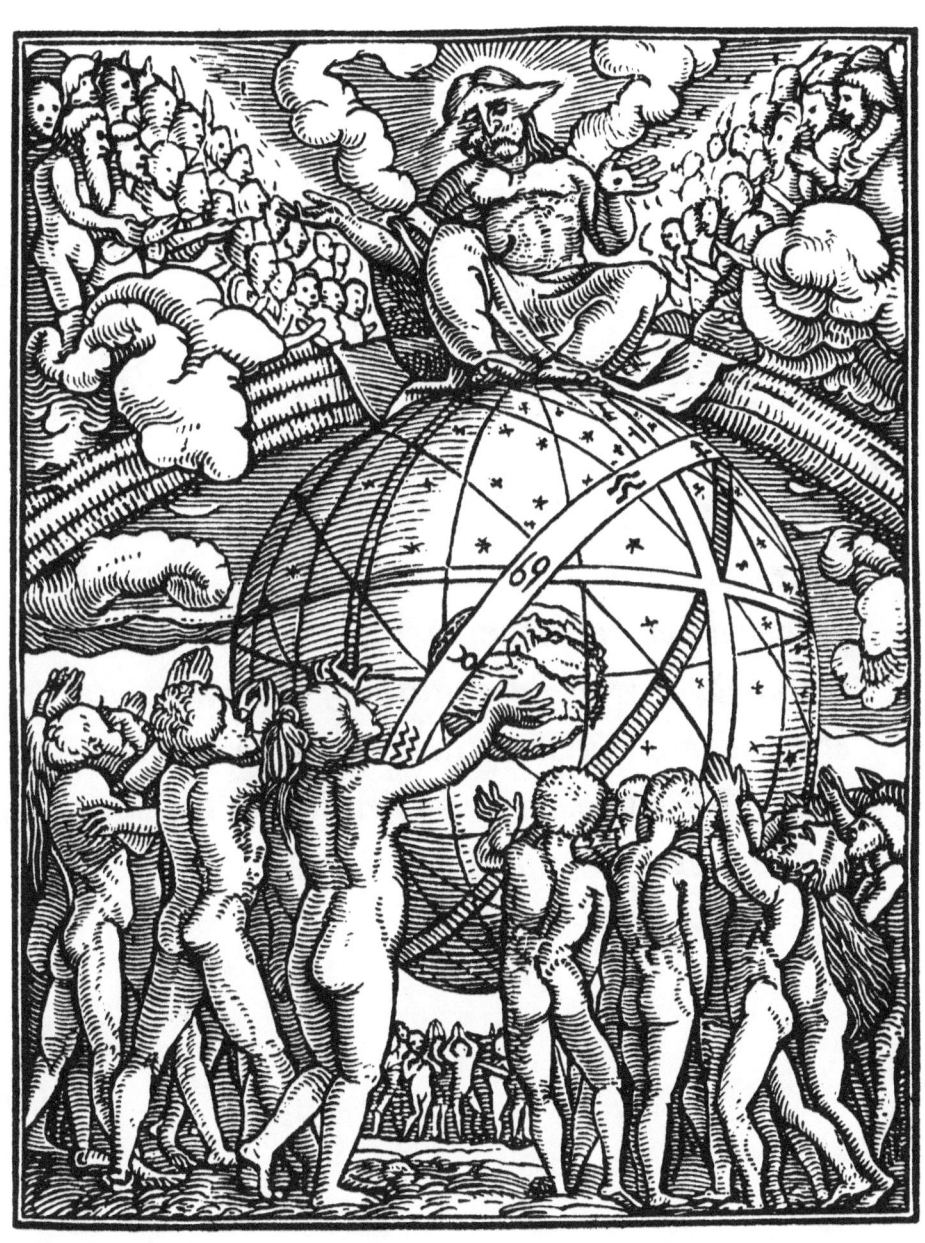

XLIX.
THE ALLEGORICAL ESCUTCHEON OF DEATH

The coat or shield is fractured in several places. On it is a skull, and at top of the crest as a helmet surmounted by two arm bones, the hands of which are grasping a ragged piece of stone, and between them is placed an hour-glass. The supports are a gentleman and lady in the dresses of the times.

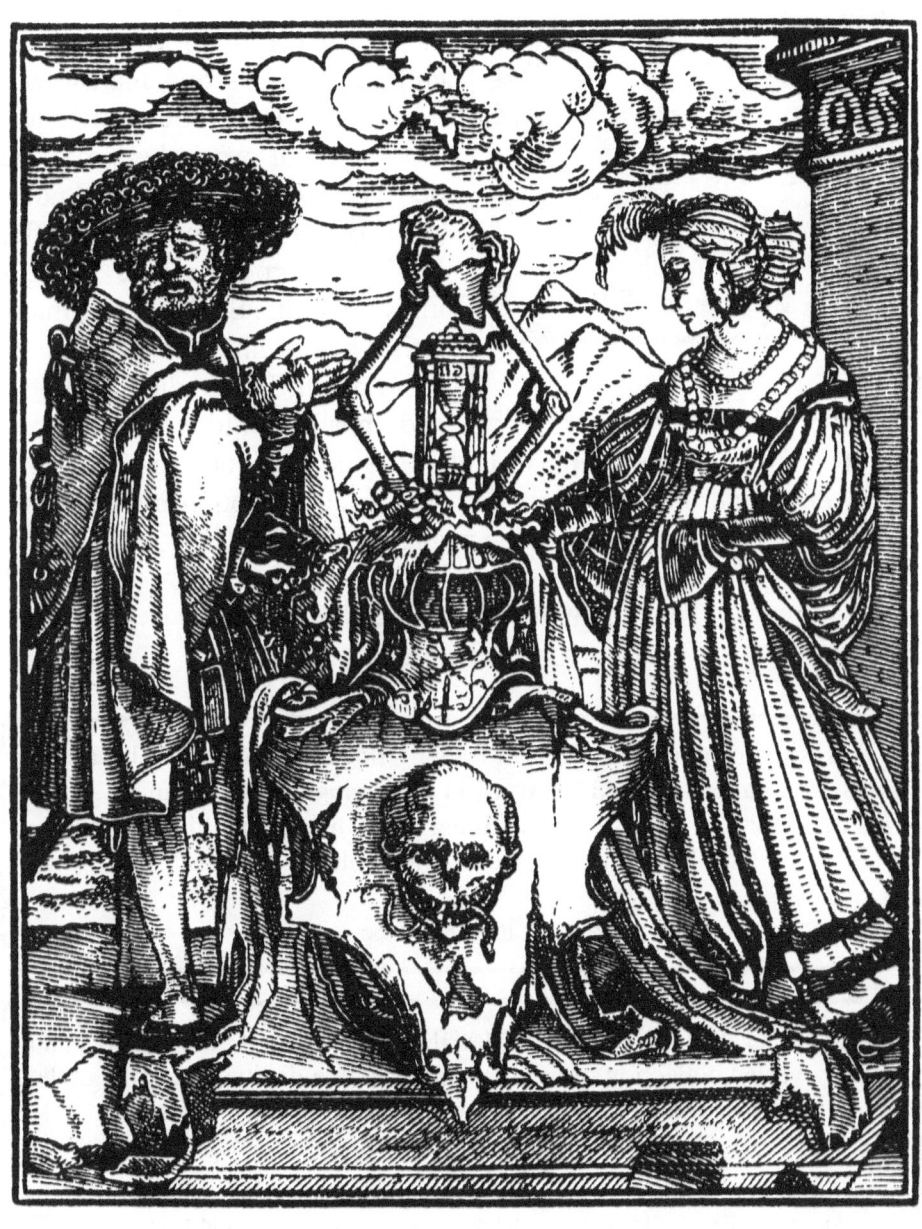

The Outlandish Art Of Mahlon Blaine

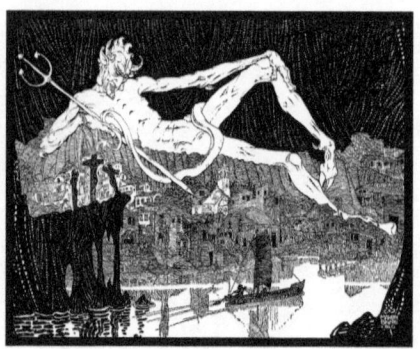

Edited by Brian J. Hunt

In 1923 Mahlon Blaine burst upon the art scene with striking works of imagination and vision. Within a short time his work was published in everything ranging from children's books and mainstream magazines to erotic portfolios. The body of work he produced between 1926 and 1930 was nothing short of phenomenal but after 1931 his output became increasingly sporadic. Sadly like so many artists before him who have given us so much, Blaine died penniless and mostly forgotten in January of 1969. This volume samples Mahlon Blaine's unique artistic visions, from his grand emergence in the roaring 20's through his declining years in the swinging 60's.

The Outlandish Art of Mahlon Blaine
http://www.mahlonblaine.com

"This is an overdue recognition of Blaine's fine eye for details in his drawings. You have presented his work in chronological order, which shows his development over the years, giving us an insight into his imaginative art. I am happy to see this fine volume in print."

-Helen de la Ree

"THE OUTLANDISH ART OF MAHLON BLAINE is an incredible and widely varied collection of a unique artist with a distinctive, gritty style. Many of Blaine's works create a delightfully creepy effect."
-Alan M. Clark

Author and illustrator; Winner of The Deathrealm Award, The International Horror Critic's Guild Award, 4 A.S.F.A. Chesley Awards, World Fantasy for Best Dark Fantasy four time winner, World Fantasy Best Body of Work, and World Fantasy Best Artist (the Howard).

www.ingramcontent.com/pod-product-compliance
Lightning Source LLC
Chambersburg PA
CBHW022106170526
45157CB00004B/1504

* 9 7 8 1 3 0 4 6 1 4 3 9 1 *